THE WIND THAT SWEPT MEXICO

THE TEXAS PAN AMERICAN SERIES

the Wind that swept Mexico

THE HISTORY OF THE MEXICAN REVOLUTION 1910–1942

text by ANITA BRENNER

184 historical photographs assembled by

GEORGE R. LEIGHTON

UNIVERSITY OF TEXAS PRESS, AUSTIN

International Standard Book Number 0-292-79024-4
Library of Congress Catalog Card Number 77-149021
Copyright 1943 by Anita Brenner and George R. Leighton;
copyright © 1971 by Anita Brenner
All rights reserved
Printed in the United States of America
Fourth Paperback Printing, 1996

Requests for permission to reproduce material from this
work should be sent to Permissions, University of Texas
Press, Box 7819, Austin, Texas 78713-7819.

⊗ The paper used in this publication meets the
minimum requirements of American National Standard
for Information Sciences—Permanence of Paper for
Printed Library Materials, ANSI Z39.48-1984.

PUBLISHER'S FOREWORD

Immediately upon its publication in 1943, *The Wind That Swept Mexico* was widely recognized as one of the most powerful and discerning pictorial histories ever published. Twenty-eight years later it is still regarded as a unique achievement.

"Only 100 pages of text and 184 historical news photographs, yet this is the Mexican Revolution in its drama, its complexity and its incompleteness!" wrote Bertram D. Wolfe in *Book Week* in 1943. "One could not have seen it more closely and fully had one taken part in it, nor could one have understood as much of its essence as Anita Brenner has managed to distill out of a lifetime of living in Mexico."

When the decision was reached to bring *The Wind That Swept Mexico* back into print, it was suggested that the story of the revolution be brought up to date. Also, Miss Brenner thought of adding a section comparing it with other revolutionary movements in the world. In the end it was decided to keep this minor classic intact and virtually unchanged. The text has been completely reset and the plates have been remade from exhibit prints kindly furnished by the New York Public Library. No other changes from the original edition have been made.

UNIVERSITY OF TEXAS PRESS

CONTENTS

THE WIND THAT SWEPT MEXICO

Winds Sweeping the World

WE ARE NOT SAFE in the United States, now[*] and henceforth, without taking Mexico into account; nor is Mexico safe disregarding us. This is something that Mexicans have long known, with dread, but that few Americans have had to look at.

We are interdependent for two reasons. The first is geography. The second is what has been happening in Mexico from 1910 to now. The first is quickly seen on the map. Mexico is a tapering continuation of the same land mass as the United States. It is the longest stretch between us and the Panama Canal, key to our defense of America's coasts. The largest, most secure deep-water harbor off California is Mexico's Magdalena Bay. Its rich oil deposits are part of the same Gulf belt that reaches from Louisiana and Texas south. All supplies moving north to us, south to the other Americas, must travel, overland, through Mexico; by sea, past Mexican

[*] 1943.

waters; the urgent traffic of the air flies depending on Mexican landing fields. Physically we are most vulnerable through Mexico—and Mexico from us. In every war in which the United States has been engaged, the enemy has bent every effort to take advantage of this Mexican vulnerability. This time, because of the kind of war it is, the goodwill of the Mexican people is itself a military objective. We are endangered to the degree that they believe we interfere with what they want.

But the relationship between us goes much farther still, because Mexico occupies a crucial position in hemisphere politics and culture. What the Mexican government does guides, in many important matters, the policies of other Latin American authorities. What the Mexican people think and feel about us is a sort of lens through which the rest of Latin America regards us. For them Mexico is a central stage on which they see their own struggles going forward. Our relations with Mexico are seen as a test of our intentions toward other peoples on this continent. Thus Mexico connects or disconnects inter-American solidarity.

The reason why Mexico has key moral prestige and provocative leadership is not size nor strength nor place; it is the Mexican Revolution, 1910 to now, the story told in this book. Most people in the United States know a great deal more about the Russian Revolution, and the Chinese, and other upheavals in this era of revolutions, than about the one next to us. It has come through dimly, confusedly, in headlined incidents: Pershing chasing Villa in the desert . . . lurid tales of religious conflict . . . scandalous reports of oil expropriations. It has not looked like that in Mexico, nor in the rest of Latin America. And it is not a finished story.

It is a living story underneath what happens in Mexico now, and tomorrow. It begins in 1910, goes through ten years of civil warfare and twenty-two of further struggle, and projects itself into the future. The phrase *la revolución*, invoked so often by two generations of Mexicans, even the children, and so common a part of the national mood and vocabulary, has many meanings. It is the past, and it is a set of beliefs. The phrase runs like a live current through everything public and personal too: politics and art and business and thought and industry and now war. Each event forecasts the next; the whole chain of events is prophetic, because the set-ups are similar, of struggles elsewhere in America. Many "North Americans" have taken and continue to take an active part in the Mexican struggle. Our government has played and continues to play a decisive role. That is why the Mexican struggle is like a nerve-center to the rest of Latin America.

Before this war is over, probably, and certainly when it is ended, there will be uprisings and upheavals in many American countries. The American Revolution set off, soon after 1776, revolutions of national independence; it was furthermore an example toward self-rule that crashed European thrones. It started something that has now spread, on a scale so colossal that it staggers the mind to grasp it, to every people and race on earth. Political freedom, as has been demonstrated here, is possible only to the extent each individual can be economically independent; and economic independence for each person is not achievable either, without political freedom. The two things have here shown themselves to be one, and though we have not gone so far toward their accomplishment as we know is necessary and possible, we have gone further than any nation. So we are the strongest, and so we have the most to lose, in this war. But the millions and millions in it with us have more to gain, and they will not stop fighting, and we will not be safe to pursue our freedoms, until they have gained theirs. To the degree they lose, ours will be menaced by the same sort of enemies. We will not be safe even on this continent, because even isolated in America the order to cease firing is not entirely in our hands.

The story of the Mexican Revolution throws up, violently, the issues being fought inside each land, within the war. It puts questions to us our government will have to meet, and is already in the midst of; questions

which the American people cannot leave safely to deals and power-barters
and accident and intrigue. Policies shaped for export have their internal
consequences. For we are not safe, either, from the inner struggles tearing
other peoples. What led to the Mexican Revolution, economically, is happening to us now. *The Wind That Swept Mexico* is the story of what followed. It is the most dramatic experience lived by an American people in
our time. And it is the story closest to us of the winds sweeping the world.

Fall of a Dictator

*I*N THE YEAR 1910 there was a Strong Man of the Americas advertised in all the world, and his name was Porfirio Díaz of Mexico. Each time he reassumed his dictatorial position the Kaiser, the Mikado, all important potentates flashed messages of joy. Financiers, industrialists, illustrious public men congratulated the Mexican people regularly on his existence. Elihu Root advised them to render Don Porfirio reverence. Writers and speakers multilingually raised him up as the salvation of his country, the stern wise parent of his people. A genius. A colossus. Inscrutable. Incomparable. Irreplaceable.

The aged man had been sitting for thirty-four years—with one brief interim—in the presidential chair. Round him, like cherubim and seraphim in a religious picture, there was a group of courtly elderly men who had long since done away with politics, devoting themselves to nourishing business.

At his right hand—pale, scrupulous, and faultless as a tailor's dream—hovered Don José Yves Limantour, primate of the holy of holies, Secretary of the Treasury. Respectfully close to the chair there knelt, bringing gifts and testimonials, a select little group of men of affairs, named the Circle of Friends of Porfirio Díaz. Near Limantour there was another little group, select too, consisting chiefly of foreigners, and nicknamed, by Americans, The Full Car. Beyond, on all sides, landowners, high Church dignitaries, heads of foreign houses, concessionaires and their prosperous Mexican advocates praised without end the blessings that flowed from *la paz porfiriana*—the Porfirian Peace.

The revolutions that had boiled for three-quarters of a century (since 1810, when Mexicans declared their independence from Spain) and that had wasted the country's substance needlessly (said the Porfirian intellectuals) were now entombed in historical volumes, printed on fine paper at the government's expense. The army's old Spanish custom of plotting to change the government had only one successful living exponent, General Díaz himself, who had practiced it on Juárez. The last try against Díaz, made in the eighties, had been picked off when the General sent a list of names to the commanding officer, wiring, "Catch in the act, kill on the spot."

Thrift, too, had clipped the military talons. Limantour controlled expenditures for arms and munitions strictly, these being expensive imports. Army bigwigs, except of course General Díaz, had been edged to the fringes of state business. As for the soldiers, they were peasants, thinking little, wanting less, living on minimal wages, and why give them more to waste on drink? Many had been recruited on personal word of some local authority—by seizure at night. Troublemakers, safely and cheaply garrisoned.

The wars for power between Church totalitarians and liberal democrats that had torn the people from 1810 to the 1870's were now appeased. The Juárez Constitution and reform laws, which had expropriated the Church, and forbidden it henceforth to own property, and closed all monasteries and convents, and reduced the clergy to the status of citizens, and even required all priests and religious to appear in public only in lay clothing, had not been abrogated. They were still the law of the land and no one had dared attempt to change it. But the President's young second wife, Doña Carmelita Romero Rubio, was a pious lady; and the President's advisers valued the resignation that the Church reinforced, teaching "Render unto Caesar . . ." So appearances were preserved, and the old Spanish maxim regarding inconvenient laws was practiced: Observe, do not fulfill.

The perfect formula for the perfect stability that money seeks had been found. It was a Strong Man with a constellation of grayed experts in business and finance, revolving around the Treasurer, and governing according to the maxim, "Little politics, much administration."

The bankers had confidence in Limantour. From time to time through the years they had stipulated, in arranging loans, that he remain in place, as guarantor of the status quo. The Limantour group, known as *los científicos* and in that name execrated by everybody locked out of the profitable circuit, had a doctrine, "Let us be scientific, let us be realistic." It was ground out solemnly in the academies, the University, the press, raisined with scholarly arguments quoted from the French physiocrats and positivists, in French, of course. It was taught in practice to the bright apprentices being groomed against the day when time, alas, should foreclose on General Díaz, and their Science would inherit full control. Democracy, the official philosophers recited, was a utopian dream, an anachronism, a plaything for rich countries. "Its bad government," Limantour remarked of the United States, "is the best proof of its greatness."

But in a land where not even fifteen per cent could read, how absurd to spend money on open elections! How visionary among a people more than ninety per cent mixed breed, dominantly Indian, racially inferior! The conquerors had indeed made a mistake—influenced by religious sentimentalisms—in allowing the creatures to live and propagate. They should have been handled as in the United States. It was now Mexico's misfortune to try to progress with such a burden upon it: more than three-fourths of the population nearly pure Indian, practically subhuman, degenerate, apathetic, irresponsible, lazy, treacherous, superstitious—destined to be a slave race. Such beings could never perform, surely could not claim, participation in the acts of government. Let them work, and keep the peace. For them the standard, *pan y palo*—Bread and Club. The government must be an aristocracy, an aristocracy of brains, technicians, wise and upright elders, scientists.

The intricacies of financial arithmetic were dull to Díaz; he left all that to Limantour, and himself ran the political machinery. He chose the governors, each one of whom—usually the biggest landowner or businessman, or an old military friend from the Juárez days—enjoyed dictatorial powers. Each one, like Díaz, had his right-hand man, the chief of police, whose organization worked smoothly toward the disappearance of malcontents and people suspected of dangerous thoughts. The methods: *pan*—a job, a few pesos, social flatteries; *palo*—blackmail; and the final alternative of the *ley fuga* (fugitive law)—"shot while attempting to escape."

A lower hierarchy, the *jefes políticos* (political chiefs), ruled the small towns. They were chosen by the governors and okayed by Díaz, and their job was to guide the municipal "authorities," operate the elections, cooperate with the secret police, and nudge the courts.

It was a safe land in which to do business. Justice was carried out according to an unwritten, unbreakable law which required that a case be settled in rigid observance of who the attorney was, who the client. Cases involving a foreigner against a Mexican were decided according to the principle that the foreigner must be right, unless word came from Don Porfirio, exceptionally, to discover otherwise. In the remotest places judges understood the fine points of these usages, and could interpret skilfully the precept taught by the U. S. State Department, that Americans were guests and must be spared the judicial annoyances unavoidable to Mexicans; that every American living and working in Mexico, from plant manager to gang foreman and oil driller, and every company that had American money in it—even if it were only one red cent, said the Embassy —had the right to this same kind of extraterritorial immunity.

Order reigned. Bullion could be transported with dozing guards, and travelers could jog along through the sun-drenched landscape, fearing no disturbance of their right of way. The peasants abased themselves before men on horseback, murmuring, hat in hand, "Go with God." The roads were patrolled by *rurales*, well-mounted active men in dove-gray uniforms, tightly buttoned with silver. They knew the trails and hideouts as well as the Indians, for many had been smugglers and ambushers, and had been persuaded into the handsome uniform by exercise of the Díaz methods. Plantation owners and the prosperous people in small communities loved them as Texas does its Rangers and Canada its Mounties. Village and hacienda workers had other emotions, since it was the *rurales* who kidnaped recruits for the army, or tied suitable prospects into the gangs shipped to the tropics—where labor was short-lived and plantation owners were willing to pay for able-bodied men at twenty-five pesos a head. Or, in general, dispense justice among the cacti according to the precepts laid down in Díaz' famous telegram.

There was music on the plazas in the evenings, and the small-towners came out to sit among the palms and listen to the waltzes and military airs. The young people promenaded, males clockwise, females in pastel muslins counter-clockwise, exchanging at the intersections meaningful silences and wadded notes of undying love. One of the benches on the plaza was always occupied by the municipal president, the judge, and the *jefe político*. As a rule he was also the local money-lender, only source of credit for small farmers, at twelve per cent and up. Most of the marketable corn and beans accumulated in his warehouse, and in combination with other *acaparadores* (monopolizers, their name in common usage) he kept supply, demand, and prices under comfortable control. This little group of solid men was sometimes joined by the parish priest, and perhaps too by a neighboring *hacendado*, who might take the pleasant occasion to transact some little business, while they sat in the incense of good cigars, and smoothed their mustaches grown plump and pointed in the Díaz fashion.

On the opposite side of the plaza there was another bench occupied by the heterodox: the doctor, the pharmacist, a lawyer maybe, the newspaper editor if there was one, the schoolteacher if any, the local telegrapher, and perhaps the barber. In some towns the priest might be the kind of man who gravitated in their direction too. Not usually, however, as it was taken for granted that these were the town's Freemasons, as well as its dreamers and odd fellows, collectors of botanical specimens and curious rocks, delvers in old papers, mouthers of obsolescent political ideas. People of no importance visited their bench. One-horse ranchers, marginal miners, shopkeepers pushed by the big-store Spaniards, ex-artisans ousted by factory goods, and spindly boys who had studied in the capital. There they sat, talking low, the old ones chewing over the Juárez days, the young ones repeating futilities heard from their fathers and teachers: democracy, free elections, municipal self-rule, lay education, independent courts, equal opportunities, citizens' rights. . . . It was evident from the way they dressed, in severe worn black, that such preoccupations led nowhere.

As far back as 1896, the last belligerently independent liberal paper, *El*

Monitor Republicano, had committed suicide. Its editor had written in fare-well: "Since there is no longer a liberal party, but only a very few men of political faith, and many degenerates, we lack a point of reference . . . Our paper, faithful observer of constitutional law, has managed to give some service defending it against the Power . . . We look for some base on which to resist, and find a vacuum . . . We furl, therefore, the remain-ing shred of constitutionalist flag . . . and wrapping ourselves in it go down to the grave of oblivion." The *Monitor* was, from a business view-point, a going concern. But it closed refusing to sell its name and fol-lowing.

There was no open challenger henceforth to the self-perpetuating Power. It was unthinkable to anyone except the shabby talkers in low key that the country would ever again hear the word "revolution," once its most common noun. Revolutions, it had been announced by Francisco Bul-nes, the brilliant orator and intellectual Cagliostro of the regime, "occur according to natural social law. And that law is that governments break down when they cannot pay their bills."

Of this condition there was not the slightest portent. The Treasury had a surplus of 62,483,119 pesos, gold. Revenues were comfortably over ex-penditures. From the time the Treasury had come into his hands, fourteen years earlier, Limantour had administered it like a business in receivership, which essentially it then was. The army appropriations had been whittled; interest payments on the foreign debt came first. Many measures had been taken to free business from feudalistic and other restraints. Internal cus-toms were abolished, taxes reapportioned. The currency, to benefit the export trade, had been put on a gold basis.

The national credit was such that smiles flowered on the faces of bank-ers floating new bonds. Through Limantour and his friend Hugo Scherer and their mutual friends in German and other European banks, Mexico had been encouraged to borrow on better and better terms. The debt had rolled from eighty million pesos to four hundred and forty million, held chiefly in Germany, and about to be consolidated at four per cent, as the crowning achievement of Limantour's career.

Railroads, to which Juárez (and Díaz when he had been a Juárez general) had once objected, fearing easy invasion from the United States, now cut important export routes, carrying ore and other raw materials free from interstate tolls. Built with government subsidies, perennially unprofitable because they served so little of the national market, the main lines had been merged through a Limantour maneuver into a national company, stock-controlled by the government, run by American management. And other industries, subsidized too, had developed by leaps and bounds. In every money market of the world investors were accustomed to regard Mexico as a bonanza land.

A dazzling future was prophesied, a golden era had arrived already, and the stock phrase was that Mexico had abandoned her turbulent, unproductive past and begun to take her rightful place among the sisterhood of modern industrial nations. Gentlefolk lived fittingly, in stone mansions, lace-hung and furnished in Louis Quinze or Directoire. They relaxed abroad in fashionable resorts; visited, with gay, exquisitely dressed parties of friends, their immense haciendas, where the manor house surrounded perhaps a half-acre of polished corridors and patios blooming with Castilian roses. Their families were intermarried with the nobilities of France and Spain. Their finances were integrated with the enterprises of German, French, British, American concerns. Their transactions were carried on elegantly, over long lunches prepared by French chefs, consummated with Rhine wines, Havana cigars, Napoleon brandy, accompanied by light Italian operatic airs.

Foreign investors, the Aladdins of expanding industry—from which would emanate all the benefits of modern civilization—were cherished. Their capital, secured by the gold standard and multiplied by government-stabilized rates of exchange, enjoyed every guarantee: tax-free concessions for ample years; customs-free machinery and supplies; subsidies; right of way in the courts; useful laws, such as those suspending the constitutional provisions (inherited from colonial days and from the Juárez charter) that had reserved subsoil resources to the nation; and above all the essential, the quintessential, guarantee, cheap and docile labor.

These were the achievements that the government of General Porfirio Díaz prepared to celebrate in the fall of 1910, as a patriotic apotheosis of one hundred years of national independence. The whole month of September was set aside as a holiday, and provision was made in the budget to make the days and nights a blazing processional of gaiety for the distinguished guests invited, all expenses paid, from every powerful nation on earth. The Plaza of the Constitution, the Cathedral, the National Palace, the avenues and boulevards were radiantly illuminated. Indians, peasants, all who showed poverty, were forbidden the central thoroughfares. The waiters who served the banquets were Europeans, or hand-picked Mexicans who could be taken for foreigners. Little girls strewed flowers in the streets, floats rolled conveying damsels in Greek draperies, holding scrolled wonderful words: *patria, progreso, industria, ciencia.* The loveliest women were brought in from the provinces. Champagne was imported in carloads for the President's Ball alone, which seven thousand guests attended.

All the evidences of culture and prosperity were displayed: the monster drainage tunnel that had freed the capital of valley floods, at enormous cost in pesos and uncounted Indian lives . . . the Renaissance post office and many other imposing government buildings . . . the electric lights in the principal cities . . . the streetcars, the telephones, the national telegraph system, the punctual railways . . . the four ports dredged and fitted up for maritime commerce . . . the industries—textiles, smelters, steel, paper . . .

the Italian marble opera house begun to commemorate this anniversary, with its fabulous glass curtain already in place, a curtain made by Tiffany at the cost of—but why count the cost? . . . Envoys presented trophies. The American Ambassador unveiled a pedestal for a statue of George Washington, counseling the Mexicans there assembled to respect and admire his spirit. But the peak—the golden brooch, as society reporters said in Spanish—of the public solemnities was the inauguration of three superb buildings, three models of Porfirian progress: a hospital, a jail, and an insane asylum.

It was a cumulative picture, dramatically unrolled, to give to foreign eyes a splendid panorama. Land of promise, exploding in bloom wherever water reached it. Land where men of imagination and money could be as Midas, and live in a paradise of natural beauties. Behold the works of some pioneers. There was the Englishman Weetman Pearson, who had built the railway connecting the two oceans, amply helped by the government; had dredged the ports, had secured the drainage-tunnel concession, and was enjoying and carrying out many other contracts. He had found oil and signed a concession, in generous partnership with the government, over the vastest rich deposits—and was now Lord Cowdray.

There was the German Hugo Scherer, intimate of Limantour. He had become connected with money in many countries and, with much pomp, embraced the Catholic faith. Through his hands had passed much of the European capital that had gone into government loans (Church money, some believed, directed from Germany through its powerful Catholic party, with the encouragement of the Kaiser, and funneled into Mexico for reasons of *realpolitik*.)

As for Americans, the invasion dreams of the nineteenth century were no longer necessary, for American industrial and agricultural enterprises were spread peacefully over the whole north and ran deep southward along both coasts. The golden tide and appetites of the eighties had jumped the Rio Grande. Guggenheim and U. S. Smelting dominated the mines, holding over ninety per cent of Mexico's most important industry. In railroads, American money far outcounted any other, and American management ran all lines except Cowdray's and a few unimportant narrow-gauge concerns. Doheny, helped by the railroaders, had energetically ridden through jungles looking for fuel, and had found it. Waters-Pierce and Standard Oil with that early start were crowding Cowdray's Dutch Shell–Eagle Oil combine. American money had absorbed plantations and ranches—cotton, sugar, timber, cattle—had developed the most profitable agricultural enterprise in the country, and now nudged for first place in this field even the Spanish, who had for generations been the lords of land. Indeed, though European money was still first in public finance and the retail trade, the dollar had long since submerged the pound and franc and peseta. The value of American holdings, virtually nothing in 1877, was gauged at $500,000,000 in 1902, and had tripled to a billion and a half dollars by 1910.

Limantour, it was true, was none too friendly to the march of the dollar, and followed a calculated policy of checks and balances, whereby dollars invested were offset by better concessions for Europeans. He practiced financially the traditional strategy by which Mexico tried to fence each hungry power, playing it off against another. Church money, forbidden by Juárez laws to accumulate in earthly property, could under his benevolent eye take cover in securities and corporations, and help dam back the dreaded liberal influences that might spread with American domination.

Still, to capital of every nationality Limantour was unquestionably a sound man, a gilt-edged guarantor of the *status quo*. And some of his best friends and even business partners were Americans, who in turn were friends of the new Ambassador, Henry Lane Wilson, who in turn had

friends and relatives in the Guggenheim, Rockefeller, and Aldrich interests; while President Taft's brother was the counsel for, and a director of,
the Cowdray oil concern.

On the whole it was a cozy little *status quo*. There was only one flaw
in it. Díaz was eighty years old, and not immortal.

In the year of the Centennial an omen appeared
in the Heavens. People who could read learned that it was Halley's Comet
and that there was nothing to fear. The scientists understood it, everything
was under control. But in the villages, where the glare destroyed the peace
of the night and made even the cattle uneasy, it was an announcement.
The young were told by the old that it meant war, death, famine, plague.

This was confirmed by word of a man named Madero, who was coming to deliver the poor and give them the land. It was understood that he
lived in the capital or some such distant foreign place, and was married
to a probably divine creature called the Constitution. Clearly he was not
the same as other city people, whom it was always best to avoid mentioning. The world of Tata Porfirio and of Doña Carmelita, who some said
was his wife (and others said nonsense, rulers do not have wives, but con-
sorts), was coming to an end. It was best to confess and commune, for the
Day of Judgment was at hand. In the center of the land roarings were
heard and ashes rained from the clouds over hundreds of miles, darkening
the sky for days. Near Tampico a pillar of fire had been seen, smoke by
day, flame by night, moving among the foreigners who said they were
digging wells.

There were old people who could remember what life had been like
before Porfirio. Many wars. There had been a great war in which the
Americans—or was it the English?—had come down from the north and,
aided by the devil, for they were Protestants and Moors, had overrun many

lands. A river had been put in, and some guards. You crossed by marking a paper saying you were going to work. In that land on the other side there was much wealth: cheap soap, many varieties of muslin. And there had been another war—or was it the same one?—when Maximiliano rode in a golden coach with Mama Carlota, and wore a crown. But Benito, an Indian with a mission, had ordered them to be killed. For they were not meant to rule in this land.

In those days there had been much corn, and prices had been half of what things cost now. Wages had been the same, of course—they never change; but people had had real silver money and could buy in the market, instead of getting everything out of a book at the hacienda store. In those days many people had had their own corn patches. But engineers had come and measured them, and it had been ruled that all the earths for which there was not the right paper must belong to the haciendas. So now the rich owned the waters and the lands, for they had sold themselves to the devil and the world was in their hands. The Lord had promised to send Somebody to do His work, and the powerful Old Ones, and Malinche, would come out then and sweep the wicked away. This was announced. Now, as could be read in the heavens, it was here.

The *científicos* were enlightened men who did not believe in omens, and were protected from this word of doom that ran among the eighty-five per cent whom they knew only as soft-footed, silent labor. But other portents were being weighed uneasily by them. In 1908 a prominent American journalist, James Creelman, had asked Don Porfirio a question no one in Mexico would have dared utter: What provision was he making for the coming years? Democracy, Díaz answered. The country had been made ready for it. He would be happy to retire at last. He would welcome real opposition in the presidential elections of 1910. It was a sensational interview. Not because of Díaz' words—that was a stock speech of Latin

American rulers to the American press—but because the question had been asked, and from the United States. Political prophets moistened a finger and held it to the wind. Was it beginning to blow from the north?

It was said, among those supposed to know, that Cowdray's American competitors, particularly Pierce, were irked, and that their powerful spokesmen in the United States would be prepared to help usher in a change of . . . policy. Those still further in the know remarked on the recent accident that had surely awakened serious struggles: the great blaze of one gusher in Tampico's Golden Lane, that roared to the sky for longer than had ever been seen, and for the first time revealed the depths and richness of the oil deposits. Harriman also was said to be most annoyed, because the railroad merger plan had been appropriated by Limantour for other beneficiaries. The Guggenheims too were said to feel badly treated by Limantour, because he had arrogantly refused to bargain with them over the sale of Mexico's richest mine, at Real del Monte (of which he owned a part), and the property had gone to other buyers.

The State Department, it was significantly murmured, was furthermore displeased by the increasing signs of affection between Díaz and Japan. A secret treaty, perhaps real, perhaps forged, had been shown in Washington, whereby Díaz granted to the Japanese sweeping concessions in Magdalena Bay in Lower California. Besides all that, the United States Government, like every other whose nationals had a heavy stake in Mexico, was concerned over the problem of the presidential succession. Díaz had a challenger no one could jail or otherwise abolish—his years.

Soon after the Creelman interview there appeared a book called *La sucesión presidencial* (The Presidential Succession) by Francisco I. Madero. It dealt with effective suffrage, no re-election, the Constitution—mostly things that had been said before, once upon a time by Díaz himself. But the author was a Madero, a younger grandson of the rich northern family

whose one hundred and seventy-two male members enjoyably increased
the fortune founded by the patriarch, Don Evaristo: some million and a
half acres in cotton, lumber, rubber, cattle; besides mines and smelters
competing with the Guggenheims; besides wine and brandy distilleries,
mortgages and real estate, and provincial banks. The Maderos were friends
of Limantour, friends too of the anti-*científico* northern businessmen
whose hope for the future was handsome, dashing General Bernardo
Reyes. And they had friends in the proper places over the border, particularly among the Cowdray competitors in railroad and banking circles.

Francisco himself, a small, quick-moving man with kind eyes, had his
portion of the Madero estates, which he seemed to be dissipating in benevolent experiments. He was a vegetarian, an ascetic, a man whose heart
was wrung by the condition of the Mexican people. The remedy, he had
come to believe, was political—the freest free democracy. Years ago he
had been a charter member, with a group of radicals, of a Liberal party
long since apparently scattered. To his family and friends he was, tolerant-
ly, "Panchito," an idealist, an innocent. The Ouija board had told him,
"Francisco, one day you will be President of Mexico." He moved to fulfill
the mandate of destiny.

The presidential term expired in 1910; the new term would begin in
October of that year. In addition to Díaz himself, the perpetual candidate,
there were three aspirants. The first was Limantour, long the heir apparent, who had been eliminated, presumably, years ago by a legal decision
disqualifying him because of his birth of debated foreign parentage. The
second was Reyes, long the hope of all the outs who had political weight:
the military, the Mexican businessmen not in the charmed circles, the foreign promoters without access to the Full Car, the large number of professionals without good jobs, the remainder of the old-time Juárez liberals,
the University students. The third perennial candidate was old Don Nico-

lás Zúñiga y Miranda, who walked the streets somberly in his Prince Albert coat, carrying a gold-headed cane, thinking up dazzling, logical presidential programs that read like satire—or madness.

And now Madero too prepared to campaign. In his first plans he aimed no higher than the vice-presidency, apparently expecting to arrive at an arrangement whereby he and his would get a portion of the Díaz government and be in line for the succession; or, if they were blocked, to make the traditional gesture of armed rebellion.

Because of the Creelman interview and the limelight of the approaching Centennial, the friends of Díaz, while attending competently to the re-election machinery, felt called upon to go through more elaborate motions. Speakers toured the principal cities. Stooge oppositions were rigged. There were mass meetings, debates in the papers, oratory in Congress. Bulnes tied fireworks to that with a speech and a phrase that was enjoyed everywhere like a vaudeville gag. "The presidential successor this country needs, gentlemen," he thundered, "the presidential successor this country wants is—the Law!" What astonished all the politicians, even Madero, was the number and energy of the Maderistas. *Jefes políticos* raised their hands bewildered, watching the parades, hearing the inflammatory speeches, seeing the identity of the leaders—birds of ill repute and omen in their sight. But orders were orders, so Fuentes the Nobody scandalized placid Aguascalientes campaigning for the governorship; and Álvaro Obregón, the mechanic and small-time rancher, stirred up Huatabampo, Sonora; and the sullen, wild-tempered peasant Emiliano Zapata brought alarmed laughter to the sugar *hacendados* of Morelos; and thus everywhere the plaza benches of the heterodox swarmed into activity like busy anthills in April.

The powerful took it for granted that Díaz would be president as long as he was alive. For them the real question was, who would be vice-president? Speculation fitted the halo to many eminent heads, but Díaz, watching ambitions come out into the open, was affably inscrutable. For days and hours, up to the last few minutes, the official nominating convention waited for the Díaz message—the Name. It came, and was voted in numbly: Ramón Corral again. Corral, who could have won the vote by acclamation as most hated man in Mexico. Corral was known as the money-maker in the Indian slave trade to the tropics, as king of another kind of slave-trade in the capital, and himself its victim, with his disease so far advanced, physicians figured, that he had at most two years to live.

"Díaz and Death"—this was the muttered name of the ticket. And the final dose, the last intolerable swallowed grievance, was that the one newspaper that received the choice with praise—the only one—was the American daily. Limantour packed up and took his family and went to live in Paris . . . to consolidate the debt. All through the Centennial dinners his official chair sat enigmatically vacant. Reyes too went off, or was sent, on a mission to study military affairs in Europe. His followers—the veteran politicians and unhappy businessmen who had set up committees, the clever professionals who had reform programs ready, the military thinking of coups, and the students who had been stirred by young Rodolfo Reyes to see a future in his father—now all took cover. The disillusioned and impatient drifted toward the Maderistas.

As for Madero, Díaz smilingly took routine precautions. Publications were suppressed, key men were jailed. Madero himself was imprisoned in a small city where, through the word of an archbishop, he was let out on bail, and escaped to the United States in the grimy costume of a brakeman. Finis. And to insure Centennial quiet, an embargo was laid on all Madero properties. Not one peso could move. The clan appealed frantically to Limantour. Other members, particularly elder brother Gustavo, took a sporting chance to stave off family ruin. He threw himself into organizing Panchito's revolution.

Of the forthcoming cataclysm there was one omen, live and menacing as smoldering Popocatépetl, and yet perceived by only a few. This was the fact that all the productive wealth of the country, the sources and the fruits, had become concentrated in a very few hands. Fewer hands even than a hundred years back, when the Spanish rule cracked, when the Church held half the wealth and the Crown had a monopoly on trade and a twenty per cent lien on all production, and when to be born in Mexico meant to be an inferior, tabooed, almost, from any high position and at galling disadvantage in any position at all.

Now, one hundred years after the revolution which had attacked those conditions, all but a fraction of the total wealth was held by about three per cent of the people. The bulk was held by less than one per cent; and most of that was in absentee foreign hands. The economic pump was making wealth flow outward, leaving behind a sediment only; and what came in, to multiply, again flowed outward. The dangerously unbalanced distribution of the means to live and produce—which wherever it occurs has always led to oppression and social explosion—had again for at least ninety-five per cent of the people of Mexico an extra taste of wormwood. There was this byword: "Mexico—mother of foreigners, stepmother of Mexicans."

No one in the government saw any cause for alarm in the narrowing ring of monopoly, except perhaps in the dominant American hold (but this, it was assumed, Limantour could handle). Industry, continuing its colonial pattern, was directed toward the extraction of raw materials for export, particularly metals, primarily silver; and silver loomed so large that the ups and downs of its market menaced all business and finance. But the over-all figures showed a great industrial increase, and a rise in that abstraction called "national wealth." Why trouble to dig behind these beautiful statistics, into their meaning for fifteen million flesh-and-blood people?

Agriculture too had increased in volume and figures showed it to be flourishing. It was rapidly taking an industrial course, and toward export products, subtracting the best lands and much labor from producing for Mexican bellies. Long-standing chronic shortages of staples—due to over-worked land, lack of water, sprawling holdings primitively worked, and many other wastages—had now become so acute that, in a land of corn and beans, corn and beans were imported. Díaz scientists, quite fully aware of a deepening agrarian crisis skirting famines, had studied and pondered and diffidently suggested remedies, which were applauded and tabled. In the long run, it was thought, industry would solve everything. By its mere existence it would create national prosperity that would sift down to the middle class, that is, the ten or fifteen per cent who were considered really people. Work would accrue to the rest, and thus the golden cycle would remain continually in motion.

But the process by which wealth was to sift down, reversing its ancient habits of traveling up, had not yet occurred. Instead, another process had been going on—a process of suction. Through it, the peasants—more than three-fourths of the population—had been stripped of land by laws which gave the *hacendados* more leeway for expansion, more water, more cheap labor. Many village and tribal holdings had been handed over, and most of the public lands, to great concessionaires, often with subsidies. Occu-pants who resisted being thus reduced to peonage were shanghaied into the army, or sold to work in the tropics, or sent to their graves.

There had been bloody Indian uprisings on this account, and the Yaquis particularly, edged to the sierra deserts by the great land companies in Sonora (dominantly American), waged suicidal war. But over half the nation's population, Indians and mestizos, were now shackled to the haciendas as peon share-croppers, rendering perpetual labor for perpetual debt, which was inherited by the sons. Some fled from time to time and became outlaws, and some were ransomed to supply railroad labor gangs, and some got over the border to work in the United States. The mass stayed silently in place, held by the hacienda priests, and by the tight rein of the *jefes políticos*, and by the *rurales*. The details of that peaceful misery come out sharply in statistics published later—an infant mortality, for instance, of more than twenty-five per cent.

One step above, the peasant-traders and artisans had also been dislocated. The weavers had been displaced by mills; the shoemakers had been left with only the sandal trade at peasant prices; the potters were now supplying the penny markets; the pack drivers, once numbered by the thousands and the backbone of the transportation system, had been decimated. They peddled along the trails with one or two burros now, getting hardly enough to feed even the burros except with the aid of a little nocturnal enterprise, as practiced by Pancho Villa and many another future revolutionary. Men drifted into the industrial centers from lost lands, lost occupations, and were there hired, and were caught in the price-rise squeeze that had come with cheapened pesos. Mexican labor, considered inferior biologically, had its wages fixed accordingly. And, though a Mexican might learn from Americans how to run a locomotive or handle smelting or oil machinery, he could never hope for more than a semi-skilled position, because of the fact that he was a Mexican.

In other lands the middle class had been swelled and benefited by the coming of industry. Here the producers and traders for the internal market lost ground as their reservoir of purchasers became steadily impoverished. The small farmers—the *rancheros*—tough and enterprising men risen from the peasantry (chiefly two generations back, by means of the Juárez laws that broke up Church and communal lands), had to compete with the great plantations, which paid scaled-down taxes, had bank credit, and were cushioned by debt-bound peon labor. The erratic Mexican climate, which makes farm credit a matter of life and death, kept the *rancheros* hamstrung by the usurers, and crop prices at the mercy of the speculators. Small miners, small manufacturers, small storekeepers faced similar conditions. Transportation was dear, tapping only the great industrial and agricultural centers. Materials were virtually inaccessible. Machinery was imported at expensive foreign prices. The tax load was weighted by innumerable petty tolls pyramided on the nobodies.

The sons of this penurious class might, through desperate family economy, manage to study law, engineering, medicine, education, art. Once graduated, to what could they look forward? In private business only the third-rate jobs were open to Mexicans, even the educated, even the blue-bloods. In the government there was a decrepit bureaucracy, and room was made for only the few who could wedge in by exercise of constant servility and ruthlessness. Even the professionals who got to the top by sheer brilliance were locked out—if they were honest men, or merely humane, or merely self-respecting—from everything connected with public administration; and everything was. The political face of monopoly—dictatorship—meant for those who lived by their brains few and fewer bottlenecked jobs.

All this had been described with cold, meticulous rage in a book called *Los grandes problemas nacionales*, published in 1909, written by a scholar named Andrés Molina Enríquez. It became to the Mexican Revolution what Rousseau's *Contrat Social* was to the French, and more. It became the gospel of thousands upon thousands of people who never heard of it, could not have read its simplest words. The book was read by scholars, professional men, students. It created a kind of intellectual climate, and provided a sympathetic grasp of the things that were exciting *rancheros* and Indian "bad men" and labor agitators.

Thus it bridged separated worlds. It lined up on the same side wealthy

liberals who had no want but political freedom, and organizers of revolutionary labor unions such as the Flores Magón brothers. They were sons of
an Indian officer of Juárez days, who, considering Díaz a betrayer, had
refused his bounty, and were now exiles in St. Louis. From there they
issued to the smelters and railroads and mills of their country blurred,
smuggled little sheets headed *Liberación*. These were irregularly published
because the editors were often in American jails (along with their I.W.W.
friends), but they reached much farther than Díaz police could erase. Students such as the Magaña brothers passed the word along to friends such
as a schoolteacher named Montaño out in Morelos, who was in touch with
the independent peasant family named Zapata, whose strapping son
Emiliano nursed a rage because the local *jefe político* had herded him into
the army (on account of a girl) and meanwhile a neighboring hacienda
had moved in on some of their village's land.

Migratory workers, startled by what they had seen of life in the United
States, came back reading *Liberación*. They got behind union drives, demanding that Mexicans receive in Mexico the same pay and opportunities
as foreigners. Their attempts to bargain collectively seldom got even so far
as strikes. And the few strikes that smudged the Díaz horizon were cut
short by slaughter. At the Greene-Cananea copper plant near the border,
American soldiers were ordered in to do the shooting.

Three occupations, Molina Enríquez had observed tartly, were open to
educated mestizos: government employment, the professions, and—revolution. The obvious conclusion was drawn. Men of tougher political consti-
tutions and better brains than Madero grouped themselves around him, the
first man of substantial name to make an open rebellious move. There were
for instance the Vázquez Gómez brothers, one a prominent lawyer, the
other a doctor who had the Díaz family among his patients. There was
Luis Cabrera, a lawyer and political scientist of Jacobin temper and the

friend of Senator Venustiano Carranza, unsuccessful bidder for the governorship of his state, who had now lost his hopes of victory via General Reyes. They had their counterparts in each small town. It was not realized then by anyone how deep and far the anger burned. For, as always when regimes collapse, the fissure showed first very close to the top.

Porfirio Díaz became President of Mexico for the eighth time on October 4, 1910. It was remarked how well he was looking. His martial, pouchy face was reassuring as ever behind his brushed, snow-white mustache. The shoulders martially square. Not a tremor in the Iron Hand. Six weeks later he was cabling Limantour urgently to come home, and small bands of guerrillas were playing tag with the Federal soldiers in the north. A few weeks after that the police machine-gunned crowds in the Plaza of the Constitution, and Díaz lay in his house in the Street of the Chain, guarded by cannon, hearing, through narcotics taken for an infected jaw, yells: "Down with Díaz! Resign! Death to Corral! Death to the *científicos!*"

Limantour, hurrying home via New York, stopped there to confer with three Maderos—Francisco's brothers Gustavo and Ernesto, and their father. The situation did not seem too desperate to him. Limantour knew how much money Gustavo Madero had managed to get his hands on— about a half-million pesos advanced by a European concern for a railroad concession. At least a third of that had gone for headquarters in the United States and to pay American lawyers. At most fifty thousand pesos—twenty-five thousand dollars—for munitions and guns. How much revolution could that produce, against the government's sixty-two-million surplus in gold, and its incomparable credit? The Maderos were panicky, anxious to come to some arrangement with him, held back from almost full surrender —and forgiveness—by Dr. Vázquez Gómez, who wanted none of that.

They made a tentative agreement, nevertheless, and Limantour went back to receive full emergency powers from Díaz, with a secret code for the Maderos in his pocket.

Conferences were arranged near Ciudad Juárez, over the border from El Paso. On hand, besides Madero kin and friends, were the Vázquez Gómez and Carranza groups, insisting on their minimum program: Díaz out, the *científicos* out, and the right to keep their boys on a military footing. "Revolutions that compromise," said Carranza stubbornly, "are revolutions lost." The conferences dragged along, Madero pleading almost in tears with Vázquez Gómez, saying his papa had promised Limantour that . . . And meanwhile the guerrillas upset all calculations. They attacked and kept on attacking. Little squads and bigger ones took garrisons and railroad junctions, and after each attack the troops snowballed in size. Cavalcades rode dustily into each captured town, headed usually by some *ranchero*, and introduced themselves to the guerrilla leaders, and joined. Some brought along their women, to take care of the wounded, and cook and forage. The dove-gray uniforms of the *rurales* began to disappear on mountain trails, and the riders with their good horses and guns appeared in Maderista hideouts. Civilians in each Maderista nucleus were fast outnumbered by men who could neither read nor write, but could ride and shoot and knew every twist of the terrain.

They had no supply line, no generals, no strategy, no organization. They just attacked, providing themselves with guns from raided stores or garrisons, or from the proceeds of looted plantations. Each leader gave his own battle orders, yelling, *"¡Viva Madero! ¡Viva la revolución!"* and in the battle the boys were on their own. Federal soldiers went through the motions of firing back, then melted away, some retreating forward and taking guns along (such as they were) to help the boys. Against Madero orders, a fairly large conglomeration led by Pascual Orozco and Pancho Villa attacked their first big objective, and took it. It was Ciudad Juárez. American soldiers were deployed menacingly along the border. Díaz messengers hurried with orders to make a deal, any deal, the best deal possible to prevent trouble with the United States and the flight of frightened capital. The jockeying began again, and the final agreement was: Díaz out. Corral out. A provisional government with U.S. confidence headed by Francisco de la Barra, Mexican Ambassador to Washington. His cabinet would be partly Maderista, partly Díaz men. They would remain about a year, call for and carry out elections, pacify the country, and . . . demobilize the revolutionary boys.

Díaz started for the coast and the German boat *Ypiranga*, waiting to carry him away. Madero started for the capital. His train took four days and nights to make a trip that normally averages thirty hours. At each station, every siding, all along the tracks, the shabby, ragged people of Mexico waited to hear him, see him, perhaps touch him. Mothers fought forward with their babies, aged and sick limped over cobblestones to the tracks, *rancheros* and peons trotted in from miles away. At dawn on the day Madero arrived in Mexico City, there was an earthquake. For the first time in generations, the spongy ground did not absorb the shock. Walls cracked, buildings crumpled, people ran praying in the streets. An omen. To Madero surely, signifying the end of a wicked era. The revolution was over. But to many others it meant the revolution had begun.

The De la Barra cabinet, one of those "governments of national unity" that in so many lands have prefaced disaster, coasted through its allotted months. Gustavo Madero worked like a beaver to salvage the old machinery and get it working just as good as new. Ernesto Madero held the Treasury with Limantour's aides and staff, and postponed the investigations and judgments that were to have made the world of business rock. In Agriculture a Maderista of good will studied projects to parcel haciendas on easy payments attractive to the *hacendados*.

The Vázquez Gómez brothers—until forced out by Gustavo—conducted the demobilization of the revolutionaries, arranging as agreed to get the guns turned in to what was left of the Federal army, but passing out other instructions and facilities privately.

In the first free elections ever held in Mexico, Francisco Madero and his running mate José María Pino Suárez were elected President and Vice-President of Mexico. Congress was turned inside out, filled with a Maderista majority and a strong Catholic bloc. In every town and village government Maderistas swept in. There was no time—though Gustavo tried—to set up a duplicate set of *jefes políticos*. The municipalities were free, the press ungagged. One could sing the national anthem and not go to jail for it. Democracy had come. And the struggles that had been going on under cover came out—and cycloned round Madero's head.

Zapata and his boys in Morelos, having been demobilized, were waiting, somehow still armed, for the distribution of lands—now. The sugar planters called mass meetings in the capital, picturing anarchy and terror in their state. Madero had gone out to reason with the Zapatistas, and while he was there an old general, Victoriano Huerta, ordered Federal troops to march upon Zapata; but the trap was blocked by quick-thinking Maderistas. In Veracruz, Reyes had arrived and, with Díaz' nephew Félix, had led a garrison revolt. It was put down and the two plotters, expecting to be shot for treason, were instead installed in a Mexico City prison, where they communicated busily with their political and military friends. In Coahuila, Carranza had refused to demobilize his boys, keeping them as state troops, quarreling with Gustavo over that expenditure, and writing the President he was a fool to disband the guerrillas. In Chihuahua, Pascual Orozco was resentfully suspicious; it seemed the silk-hat Maderistas were getting the rewards for which the ragged ones had fought. Encouragement to rebel, and money for arms, reached him from the great landlords (particularly the Terrazas family) and he rose, advising Zapata that this was a continuation of the revolution, in the name of Zapata's program. He rebelled too, and troops went out against both of them. Andrés Molina Enríquez had put the rage of the guerrillas in words, issuing a manifesto, the *Plan de Texcoco*, which said the revolution was being betrayed, and outlined what to do and demand, and this became the base of Zapata's *Plan de Ayala* and the marrow of all revolutionary demands henceforth; and he was jailed.

Ambassador Wilson dined every day with the Foreign Minister, pressing claims, demanding damages. Every bill for property and life lost that was being presented by law firms close to him, including claims for Germans, Spaniards, Belgians, French, and Chinese, he made his official business. The oil companies were angry too. And Lord Cowdray had arrived in person to dispose of this Madero nonsense about collecting the government's share in his concessions. Ambassador Wilson was cabling Washington constantly, in substance: "There is no peace, there is no order, the rabble is rising, this government cannot stand, the man is mad . . ." and American troops were called out along the border—the move that had panicked Díaz. Said Madero piteously to the newspaperman Edward Bell: "Why does your government persecute me? Why does it put its heel upon me, and grind me down like a worm?"

The Díaz army, fighting guerrillas for Madero now, scattered even faster than before. Pascual Orozco was bearing down on the capital, Zapata was harassing it from the south. The tough old Indian-killer Victoriano Huerta begged for and received command of the northern campaign and swept back the Orozco revolutionaries. Gentlefolk smiled and breathed more freely. A Strong Man had arisen. It was only necessary now for the generals to get together with the right *políticos*, and solidify with the proper foreign support. Absurd, said Madero when the plans and lists of those involved in the new plot—most of the army heads—were brought to him. Ridiculous. What could a few reactionaries do to him, the choice and symbol of the people?

In February, 1913, just fifteen months after Madero became President, the plotting generals struck, from within the *Ciudadela*, Mexico City's garrison. They got Reyes and Félix Díaz out of prison and moved on the National Palace, where the officers were in the plot. But Gustavo got there first, and theatrically made a clowning, reckless speech to the troops, dividing them. Then the post commander, General Villar, in bed with a crippled leg, somehow reached the Palace too, and when Reyes and Félix Díaz and their troops arrived they got bullets instead of *vivas*. It was a wild and furious scramble, in which Reyes was killed and Villar gravely wounded. Huerta then asked for command of the government defense and Madero said yes, though Villar, hoarse and almost incoherent, gasped no.

Ten days of battle, "The Tragic Ten," followed. From the *Ciudadela* Díaz and General Mondragón cannonaded the Palace, about a mile through the heart of town, and the population crouched indoors under mattresses. Machine-gunners and snipers cut into the defense with strange accuracy; one whole column of government *rurales*, for instance, was marched directly into the *Ciudadela* line of fire, and wiped out. On the edge of the city General Blanquet sat tight, refusing to bring his troops in as reinforcements; the soldiers, Huerta explained to Madero, were thought untrustworthy. Ambassador Wilson came around continuously to scold Madero, and insist that this disorder, this carnage, cease at once. What seemed to concern Madero's advisers most was that the revolutionary boys be kept out of the fight, so Madero hurried out to Morelos to see Zapata, to beg him not to move, and Zapata promised.

Every home was in a state of siege. Civilians dodging out for food were often caught in crossfires, and their bodies lay in the streets. Women ran on desperate errands carrying white flags made of sheets tied to brooms. The capital was paralyzed. A million people had become only a battlefield. The Embassy car circulated in the city with an enormous American flag. Its occupant was bound on errands of mercy and . . . here and there he

talked to *Ciudadela* delegates such as Reyes' son Rodolfo, and to Senate leaders of the Catholic bloc, and to aides of Huerta. A secret printing press, that the diplomatic corps thought was in the cellar of the Embassy, issued leaflets urging support for the attacking generals.

On the tenth night Huerta invited Gustavo Madero to supper. From that table he was taken to Félix Díaz and Mondragón in the *Ciudadela*, and there at dawn, together with the chief of the Palace guards, he was drunkenly lynched. Meanwhile Blanquet and his aides seized the President, the Vice-President, and one loyal general, Felipe Ángeles, and put them under guard in the Palace. And meanwhile Ambassador Wilson called the diplomats together in the Embassy and read them the list of the new government, which had been arranged in a nearby room. Huerta was introduced. He would be provisional president, and the cabinet would be partly *Ciudadela* crowd and partly men of confidence such as De la Barra and Jorge Vera Estañol, attorney for over forty important American and other foreign interests. The Ambassador embraced Huerta and proposed a toast to the new government of law and order. Church bells clamored, ringing joyfully in all the spires. Te Deums were ordered sung.

And what, asked the Cuban envoy, Manuel Márquez Sterling, would happen to Madero? The Ambassador shrugged. After all, it must be remembered, he said, that he was the dean of the diplomatic corps and could not meddle in internal Mexican affairs. A Chilean diplomat hurried to the Palace and got to the room where the President was imprisoned, and refused to leave. A proposal arrived from Huerta: if Madero and Pino Suárez resigned, their lives would be spared. The resignation was written and sent, and the Chilean diplomat waited for the escort that was to take Madero to his train. It did not come. Rolled up in a blanket and stretched out on two chairs, the Chilean diplomat went to sleep; and in the morning, still no escort came. Madero's wife begged Ambassador Wilson to send a message to President Taft, asking for sanctuary. No answer ever came.

In Texas the legislature rushed petitions to Washington, to get President Taft to do something to save Madero's life, saying he was a humane and democratic man, much misunderstood.

On the night of Washington's birthday, three days after the Pact of the Embassy, Madero and Pino Suárez were removed from the Palace and taken somewhere—to the stables, said one of the police gang later—and there "shot while attempting to escape." Their bodies were found dumped outside the walls of the model penitentiary.

The revolution, Ambassador Wilson advised Secretary Knox, was finished. Huerta was being installed with all due process of law by the Senate, and the leading foreign governments, the Germans, the British, the Spanish, had quickly recognized his rule. He requested that his own pledge be officially corroborated. But, since the Taft Administration had only two weeks left, the problem was nervously left to Woodrow Wilson and his incoming Democrats. The Ambassador worked meanwhile to stabilize the new regime. He wired all American consuls in Mexico asking them to use their influence to persuade local authorities to submit to Huerta, telling them that all other governors and municipal bodies had already done so.

The message was not in every case convincing. Some of the boys, undemobilized, had a wild-throated, baying answer: *"¡Viva Madero! . . . ¡Muera Huerta! . . . ¡Mueran los gringos! . . . ¡Viva la revolución! . . ."*

Upheaval

HUERTA, THE MASK-FACED MAN whom Ambassador Wilson ushered to the presidential chair in February, 1913, brought sweet sleep to the right people. This elderly Indian saloon tough had earned his army rank killing Indians for Díaz, but he had never counted for much among the politicians or the military. The Strong Man build-up began for Huerta when he swung troops against Zapata, almost successfully trapping Madero; when he came back victorious over Orozco, he was military leader Number One. That made him Ace of Spades in the political game. In the "Ten Tragic Days" he had outplayed both his military friends and the Maderistas, and had raked in the backing of the foreigners, the high clergy, all the big money. Clearly, here was a contractor equipped to nail the Díaz system in again. A true Strong Man, a killer with cunning.

Since Mexican governments stand or fall ultimately according to what is decided in Washington, it was first necessary to convince President Taft that Huerta's position was in accord with due process of law and to show the incoming Wilsonian Democrats that the Mexican people were very happy to have had Madero removed and Huerta elevated. At the same time the Mexicans had to be shown that Huerta was their man—had the strongest backing, had access to money, and was approved by high men in all the civilized world. All hands rallied to the job. Sermons extolled the Huerta peace. Bankers prepared to make funds available. The Church lent a million pesos. The Kaiser sent word that Huerta was "a brave soldier, who would save his country with the sword of honor." The leading cigarette company, French-Mexican, wrapped up a new brand with Huerta's face on it suitably framed in laurels. The American ambassador reported to Washington that state and municipal authorities had accepted Huerta unanimously.

Perhaps it wasn't worth while mentioning that in Coahuila, where Carranza was governor, the legislature was protesting openly that Huerta's elevation was unconstitutional. Nor that in Aguascalientes and other states, governors and municipal presidents were making their arrangements with Carranza. Nor that in Sonora, where the governor had discreetly gone away, Obregón, Hill, and other Maderista authorities and leaders were saddling up. Nor that in Morelos the Zapatistas were so unpacified that the new government planned, it was announced, to remove them all and resettle the state with shiploads of Japanese.

For his part, the ersatz Díaz picked up old Porfirio's formula and applied it wholesale: submit and be rewarded, or disappear forcibly. There was a boom in government business. Mondragón, the Minister of War, in partnership with one of Huerta's sons, earned in commissions (as figured by an employee of the department) some three and a half million pesos in four months on goods they bought for the War Department. The National Treasurer, according to the memoirs of an insider, "sacked the Treasury and all the public offices, stealing personally more than two million pesos."

Huerta sat every day dispatching state business from behind a cognac bottle in his favorite bar, the Café Colón, a place with conveniently furnished dining rooms backstairs. In the evenings the government moved to his "rabbit hutch" outside the city. "I always found him," said Rodolfo Reyes, the Minister of Justice, "in strange company, eating national dishes . . . singing . . . and acutely alcoholic." Every night the police trusties convoyed oppositionists, or people who knew something, or were in somebody's way, or had the wrong women, in cars to the suburbs, and there ended the ride.

President Wilson waited some weeks to make up his mind. Then he recalled the Ambassador and said flatly, "Huerta must go." He laid down the conditions: free elections in which Huerta must not be a candidate, and pacification of the country.

If these were met, the American government would look with friendly eyes on arrangements for a loan. If not, no loan would be forthcoming from anywhere. This brought a dignified, flowery reply from Gamboa, previously known as a writer of spicy novels, who was pinch-hitting as Huerta's Foreign Minister; there was pained, disdainful comment on Wilson's ideas in the London press. In spite of the Wilson boycott a loan was arranged in Europe, amounting to sixteen million pounds in bonds, which, after commissions, expenses, and previous commitments had been deducted, netted Huerta seven million pesos. He began to levy on business houses directly. The surplus accumulated in the days of Díaz was long gone, and the local banks were beginning to need moratoriums themselves.

Congress—the same congress produced by the Maderista elections—assembled in October, 1913. Dramatic inquiries were to be held, and data heard, regarding murders and disappearances: a deputy, a senator, other prominent politicos, "obstructive" newspapermen. The building was surrounded by troops and police, and one hundred and ten lawmakers were marched off to jail. The next morning Sir Lionel Carden, Britain's new ambassador and good friend of Lord Cowdray, ceremoniously presented his credentials. Mrs. Edith O'Shaughnessy, wife of the American chargé d'affaires, wrote in her diary: "It appears there was quite a love-feast; Huerta, of course, was immensely pleased at the proof of recognition at the delicate moment of his birth and first struggling cry as dictator."

The representatives, said Mrs. O'Shaughnessy, had been "in session, conspiring against their constitution." Their mothers, wives, and daughters went to the Embassy "in a constant stream . . . for help, though of course we can do nothing . . . They fear the Deputies will be shot, but I hardly think shrewd old Huerta will go to any unnecessary lengths . . . He didn't arrest members of the Catholic party who, for the most part, had been trying to sustain order through him . . . The Senate he simply dissolved. They have not been giving him so much trouble." Two days later she put down, "Proofs multiply of direct conspiracy of the Deputies against the provisional government. If you scratch a Maderista Deputy you are sure to find a revolutionary of some sort. The task of establishing peace seems well-nigh hopeless." And after that she concluded, "Huerta has very little natural regard for human life. This isn't a specialty of successful dictators, anyway. Only by the hand of iron can this passionate, tenacious, mysterious, gifted, undisciplined race, composed of countless unlike elements, be kept in order. In the States . . . this isn't quite understood."

This was a faithful reflection of what was being said in the powerful embassies and at fashionable receptions, by all the right people. But President Wilson had sent his own leg-man, Governor Lind of Minnesota, an untailored democrat who had not been converted. So Secretary of State Bryan telegraphed all American consuls: "Usurpations like that of General Huerta menace the peace and development of America as nothing else could. . . . It is the purpose of the United States therefore to discredit and defeat such usurpations whenever they occur. . . . If General Huerta does not retire by force of circumstances it will become the duty of the United States to use less peaceful means to put him out."

The substance of these instructions, thoroughly publicized in Mexico, sent a wave of apprehension over the people. The German envoy, Admiral von Hintze, said smilingly to Mrs. O'Shaughnessy that the United States was not prepared for war: "You can't make soldiers overnight." But for Mexicans the meaning seemed to be, the United States is getting ready to march in. For the first time Huerta, who was pictured in undercover cartoons as a death's head with a cognac glass, had a taste of something else —popular sympathy.

There were no hurrahs for President Wilson among the revolutionaries. The only thing marked "Made in the U.S.A." they wanted was guns, with which to do the job on Huerta themselves.

First among them—but by courtesy only, and just because he had been the first to issue a formal call against Huerta in the name of the Constitution—was the white-bearded Venustiano Carranza of Coahuila. He controlled the northeast corner of Mexico, which included the most convenient gun-running territory, and was near the strategic junctions of the railroads to the capital and to the oil-fields. His leading brain truster was Luis Cabrera, who believed that American capital should be curbed by stiff competition from other sources and that all foreign capital should leave a sizable slice of the benefits in Mexico. He wanted the revolution to cut into monopoly, curb the church as Juárez had done, destroy the remains of feudalism, and back a new, strong middle class—business men, industrialists, professionals, and small farmers. Carranza had been a senator in the Díaz days. He was a cold-eyed, sensual, stubborn old patriot who believed himself to be the only possible savior of his country, a superman. He gave himself the title of First Chief and fought implacably to enforce it.

To the northwest, in Chihuahua and Durango, was Pancho Villa, the former cattle rustler and pack driver. Sometimes he obeyed Carranza, sometimes he didn't. He had rolled up a phenomenal record of victories since the fight against Díaz had begun and by now had a little council building him up as the future Strong Man. He had a foreign affairs department in the person of George C. Carothers, President Wilson's agent. He had a financial advisor who, it was assumed, was in touch with the Terrazas clan and with Hearst and other interested Americans. As a counsellor of policy and teacher of Clausewitz, Villa had General Felipe Ángeles, who hoped that law and order might be established not too far to the left. General Ángeles had attachés of his own, including the artist Francisco Goitia, whose job was to paint, as he went along, the triumphs and agonies of the revolution. Above all, Villa had the feared and famous —it seemed invincible—Dorado cavalry.

To the southwest, in Morelos and Guerrero, was Emiliano Zapata, called "The Attila of the South" by the newspapers of Mexico City. He operated in complete independence of the other revolutionaries and his council had no middle grounders at all. With him were an eloquent lawyer, Antonio Díaz Soto y Gama, and the Magaña boys who had agitated the college students, and the village schoolteacher Otilio Montaño, who had written in grim clumsy rhetoric the first formal revolutionary program—Zapata's *Plan de Ayala*, derived from Molina Enríquez' ideas and preaching complete, immediate expropriation of lands and other productive holdings for the benefit of the poor. The slogan "Land and liberty" didn't mean the acquisition of these things gradually and in the future; it meant land and liberty by direct action right now.

The only military chief who was his own brain trust was a *ranchero* and ex-mechanic from Sonora in the northwest, the plump and agreeable Álvaro Obregón. His personal followers were the fiercest fighters in Mexico, Yaqui Indians. He considered himself a socialist and was unique among the guerrillas in the way he ran campaigns. Before each major move he talked things over with his staff, taking stock of details in his remarkable photographic memory. Political matters he worked out with friends such as the other "socialist" generals—Hill, Alvarado, and Calles—and civilians who were mostly labor organizers and a few intellectuals connected with unions in some way. What Obregón decided to do was always a combination of desirables with practicables, in terms of the circumstances and people involved—that is, a shrewd, immediate political adaptation of the boys' radical demands.

These four men, with their armies and retinues, were the great guerrilla chieftains. In addition there were scores of other chieftains who, with a few hundred followers, acknowledged bigger leaders only provisionally, and there were still others trooping independently who recognized no overlordship whatever. The first and indispensable requirement of a chief was that he had proved himself without fear in battle. The second was that he be a winner, and the third, that he be generous with the proceeds. They campaigned like tribes, each chief with his bunch of boys, sometimes allied loosely with other chiefs, sometimes following super-chiefs, picked according to their successes and the material returns on these. The battle cry was "*¡Qué viva Villa!*" . . . *¡Qué viva!* whoever the chief might be, followed by a hoarse, growling, shrilling "*¡Qué viva la revolución!*"

There was no agreement binding the revolutionaries. There was only a common enemy—Huerta—and a common drive to get a satisfactory place in life. And as the revolutionary wave began to roll—"Death to Huerta, down with the foreigners, Mexico for the Mexicans"—there was revealed also an unarticulated set of common hates which could be seen operating when a revolutionary army came to town.

First the jails were opened and the prisoners invited to join. Next a loan was levied on the local rich, except in the rare case of a rich man who was also a sympathizer. Goods were taken from the stores too, and here the line drawn was between Mexicans and foreigners, but in exact reverse of the distinction made in Díaz days. Some chiefs issued receipts for what was taken and conducted the disgorging of stores and warehouses in a formal, systematic way. Mostly, however, it was done with a yell— "That one's a Spaniard!"—and the stuff was taken by whichever soldiers were there first, enthusiastically helped by the store's former customers. Food and liquor went at once in long, hilarious parties with music: songs about love, hunger, jail, and exile, punctuated with shots at times, to decide impromptu who was brave and who wasn't. You could sometimes tell whose soldiers they were by the songs. Villistas tore loose about *Adelita*, "green as the sea were her eyes . . ." Carrancistas strung bawdy rhymes about politics and women to the chorus of *La Cucaracha*, the cockroach who couldn't travel any more. Zapata's men sang in melting tenor to *Valentina*, breaking to sudden ear-piercing whoops with "If I am to die tomorrow, let them kill me right away . . ." The next day was a town fair: a bunch of ostrich plumes exchanged for a Christ Child out of a church, perhaps, or a good cursing parrot for a mother-of-pearl-incrusted gun.

The fighting style of the troops became a projection of each region's kind of daily life. Some were *ranchero* units, based on the farm owned by the chief, or perhaps on a captured ranch, or on a hideout in the sierra neighborhood. Each had started round a core of the home-town or home-farm boys. In Guerrero, for instance, the Almazán brothers, medical students of *ranchero* family, led off a unit of the local farmhands. In the village of Jiquilpan in Michoacán, young Lázaro Cárdenas, who had a little job as some sort of court clerk, opened the village jail and took its single prisoner away with him to find or make the nearest guerrilla troop. In some of the most arid places a few parish priests, perhaps remembering that the revolutionary heroes of generations past had been such men as they, unfrocked themselves and joined their rebel congregations. As a rule the general staff of each segment or troop or division consisted of two kinds of people: *rancheros* or independent peasants, and professionals— the young doctors, lawyers, writers, artists, druggists, telegraphers, engineers—who had sat smoldering on the discounted plaza bench.

The Zapatistas were a revolving peasant army, based on their own homes. The soldiers went back from time to time to look after their corn and chile patches. A detachment could often, if in a bad military spot, simply evaporate, each man becoming again a soft-eyed, vague-talking peasant by just slipping off his cartridge belt and putting it with his gun in a cache. It was impossible to defeat them, difficult even to find them, as they materialized only when they were ready to attack; and knew, besides, all the shortcuts in their mountain country and the tunnels and caves used by runners, soldiers, and spies since before Moctezuma. They wore ordinary peasant white, except the chiefs, who dressed in *ranchero* clothes; in Zapata's case symbolic, theatrical dead-black, skintight and set off with startling silver. Under the great hat his face was small, Asiatic, sensuous. Mandarin mustaches drooped over his full red lips, and his soft cat eyes looked out, as in a mask of skin, from the death's head of his skull. The first act on raiding an hacienda or municipal center was sharp and symbolic; they got to the safe and destroyed all papers dealing with land titles, and then invited the neighborhood peasants to homestead on the hacienda lands.

The northern revolutionaries had a more military look. They wore uniforms, or parts of them—khaki bought in the United States, and broad-brimmed Texas hats—supplemented with job-lot accessories. One division wore magenta socks; there was a battalion with silk bandannas and a brigade in orchid shirts. The cavalrymen wore mostly tight *ranchero* pants and military tunics. There were some troops of sierra Indians, braves in loincloths with a hawk look on their faces, carrying six-foot bows.

The main battles were along the railroads, with advance attacks often carried out in combination with railroad men who had waived their pay-roll and pension rights and had come in as revolutionaries. A locomotive might be speeded ahead, heavily armed, moving fast into a town like a tank; or an old engine or a handcar might be turned into a torpedo by loading it with explosives and sending it crashing into a Federal train.

When these armies moved it was like a mass migration. They carried families, three layers deep: some inside the boxcars, some on top, and others, mostly the boys and young men, in hammocks slung between the wheels. Tortillas were ground and baked on fires in oil cans along the whole top of the train, and dogs and babies accommodated themselves in the warmest corners inside. The age span for soldiering was from about seven to seventy. Boys under ten were usually buglers, drummers, or couriers, and did sentry duty too. Beyond twelve no one questioned their place as full-fledged soldiers. The women, though their job was foraging, cooking, and looking after the wounded, pitched in and fought if they felt like it. If a woman's husband was killed, she could either attach herself to some other man or take over his uniform and gun herself. Almost every troop had a famous lady colonel or lady captain, a husky, earringed girl armed to the teeth, and among headlong, reckless fighters one of the first. All these people, Zapatistas, followers of Obregón or Carranza, painters and buglers, Yaqui Indians and mule drivers, were known as Constitution-alists—opposed to the Federals whose reluctant bayonets upheld Huerta. Within a year, despite all international calculations to the contrary, they had wiped the Federals out in three-fourths of Mexico.

By April, 1914, the Huerta dictatorship was left with only the capital and a small piece of Mexico open toward the Gulf —the oil coast. There were in the Gulf already many signs of the war that was being prepared in Europe—British, German, Dutch, and American ships hovering around Tampico. The German boat *Ypiranga* was navigating cautiously toward that port with a cargo of guns and munitions for Huerta. As the rebels neared Tampico a delegation of consuls went out to meet them, to ask that they delay their attack a few days, while preparations were made to safeguard foreign life and property. The rebels said no, and got ready to attack.

Who would govern Mexico for how long, and above all who would control the oil pumps, was now a question desperate enough to rip all protocols. Some American marines who came ashore for water, presumably, were arrested by Huerta soldiers, held, and later released with apologies. Not the proper apologies, it appeared, for the United States wanted a formal naval salute, and how much salute and what kind became the apparent core of an angry dispute. Meanwhile the rebels attacked and took Tampico, and the *Ypiranga* scuttled around and headed for Veracruz. And meanwhile President Wilson had asked Congress to authorize Secretary Daniels to send a fleet to Veracruz. Admiral Fletcher was cruising conveniently near, so he got there before the *Ypiranga*, seized the port, and occupied the city forcibly, proclaiming martial law.

The nightmare of Mexico was fact in Veracruz. "We are being invaded! . . . *¡Viva México!* Death to the gringos! *¡Qué viva la revolución!*" Hate broke loose in riots everywhere. American flags were torn, stamped in gutters, consulates and business houses were stoned, all fair-skinned, foreign-speaking people had to wear identifying lapel-flags—anything but the Stars and Stripes—or be hustled about by mobs. Trainloads of refugees fled to the ports or to the capital, intercepted often by gangs who did with the travelers as they saw fit. There was much distress and humiliation, surprisingly few deaths. But henceforth Americans, who had been the *civis romanus sum* in Díaz days, remained as barely tolerated aliens, each one's position as good only as his neighbors' opinion of him and his record with the people working with him.

There was now, from Washington's point of view, no government in

Mexico. Huerta severed relations and sent Chargé d'Affaires O'Shaughnessy off to Veracruz, escorted by Huerta Junior. Carranza proclaimed that the occupation was a shameful violation of national sovereignty and demanded that the Americans withdraw at once. Villa sent word, through Mr. Carothers, that he wasn't angry, for "Huerta must not be allowed to use his satanic abilities to start a war with the United States." Mr. Carothers tried to negotiate with Carranza to declare the oil zone neutral territory so that the oil men could come back to the wells. Carranza said they could come when they liked; his government was in full control and there was nothing to prevent them from working.

A batch of Pan-American diplomats sat down at Niagara Falls with a delegation of Díaz-Huerta envoys in frock coats to design a future for Mexico. When the rebels got astride the main railroad line to the capital and Huerta began to pack, Secretary of State Bryan sent the Niagara Falls talkers a message saying that he thought the Constitutionalists were going to win and that any provisional government decided upon must be "actually, avowedly, and sincerely in favor of the agrarian and political reforms" wanted by the revolution. Carranza observers asked the Americans at Niagara Falls when the United States was going to stop interfering in Mexican affairs, and let their case rest. Germany shifted envoys, replacing Admiral von Hintze, who had been on such cordial terms with Henry Lane Wilson and Huerta, with another naval nobleman, who soon became one of Carranza's best friends.

In July, 1914, the *Ypiranga* nosed in and took Huerta aboard, and the Constitutionalists marched into the capital. What was left of the Federal Army was demobilized and the revolutionary troops formally took its place. Washington sent messages of warning, telling Carranza he would be held responsible for damage and loss of life. Messages of advice were sent too, saying that it would be a good idea to make some arrangement with Zapata, and that there was an American agent there ready to help along. Carranza replied he would take care of these matters himself.

This was his reply also to every proposal, suggestion, and demand that came from within Mexico. The revolution, Carranza said, was finished. Mexico would now proceed, under his guidance as Supreme Chief, into orderly and prosperous life. Elections would be held soon to change provisional into regular tenure. All the boys except those needed for a standing army could begin turning in their guns and go back to work. The lawless elements that had been moving in on the haciendas would have to get out and settle their grievances in the courts. Industrial workers who had been calling strikes and making demands would have to realize that labor could not be allowed to dictate to management. In due course, progressive laws would be passed to safeguard elections and bring on the common welfare.

But the revolutionary chiefs and their boys did not see in the bony, elderly man with the long white beard the Saint Peter to their heaven. He was First Chief by their will, for their benefit. The separate worlds of Indians and white, master and servant, city and corn patch, that had been Mexico since the conquest, had been hurled together and the biggest part now knew something never felt before—its power. They had started with nothing and fought their way up to undisputed victory. They had broken the yoke themselves and now all the good things of Mexican life would be theirs—starting at once. Else what was a revolution?

Carranza's answer was—obey. A convention of generals was called in Mexico City; it cheered Carranza and endorsed him as president. But Villa had refused to attend, and Zapata didn't come either. Zapata said flatly that he would demobilize his boys the instant Carranza made the *Plan de Ayala* the base of the new government's program.

Obregón and his friends in the Villa and Carranza camps arranged another convention in Aguascalientes, halfway between the two headquar-

ters. Villa moved his troops up and turned the convention into a demon-
stration of strength. The town gaped as the powerful, thick-jawed man with
the flicking animal eyes danced his horse up and down the reviewing lines.
The famous Dorado cavalry galloped past, and the infantry kicked up the
dust, and the Indians stalked solemnly by, and there was an airplane too,
that sputtered and roared and circled miraculously in the sky. The convention decided: Carranza would retire, Villa too. The convention's choice
for provisional president was General Eulalio Gutiérrez, nobody's man
and no power in his own right. Carranza and Villa both sent dramatic
messages, saying they would yield everything if the assemblage believed
that they were malignant obstacles to the national welfare. Villa furthermore offered, if that was the consensus, to have himself shot. Neither,
though, would yield anything until the other had done so first. The convention fell apart: each general chose between the two chiefs. The majority went to Villa; Obregón and his friends in the two camps—the left-
wingers and laborites—deliberated. Fearing Villa's animal instabilities,
and the identity of his backers, and the amount of armed power in his
hands, more than Carranza's petulant despotism, they sided with Carranza.

Five years of warfare followed. The battleground was everywhere, and
every inhabitant became accustomed to living provisionally, and to being
ready to migrate fast, in the wake of one army or away from another, to
get food. There were nearly two hundred kinds of worthless paper money.
The orthodox private-property men who were Carranza's chief advisers
found seizing funds and other necessaries a disorganized way of running
an army—which, besides, set a dangerous example. So a printing press
traveled with the general staff to make money, and thus, explained the
theoreticians, "all the people shared the opportunity of financing the re-
vindicating Constitutionalist revolution." This struck a great many other
chieftains as a good idea, so they issued currencies too; Zapata naïvely
had his official pesos hacked out of pure gold and silver bullion. The

moment a general took a town, only his script was legal tender, good for just the time he held on. Buying anything and everything became the frantic occupation of troops and non-combatants, prices ballooned grotesquely, and food or any goods could be coaxed only through barter, or with gold or gun in hand. The *bola*—the guerrilla fighting—was now the only way to get ahead; and many thousands more whose jobs and wages now meant nothing, attached themselves to whatever troop swept through.

The railroads, prime military objectives, were torn up and patched and blown up and fixed and torn up again. A mountain of scorched and buckled scrap rose in the central yards at Aguascalientes. The tinted walls on almost any street in every town were pocked with bullet holes, and the best houses gaped roofless, and quail or coyotes nested inside. The spatter of rifle-fire disposing of some *hacendado* or other rich man who had hidden himself or his money was a familiar sound of the night, like an owl's cry. Hanged men hung desiccated, tattering like scarecrows, in many wooded spots, and Sunday sightseers strolled out to look, and sometimes enterprising villagers put up refreshment stands. Typhus, as in most wars, killed many more than bullets; and the diseases endemic among the forgotten eighty per cent became epidemics. Life had to be used today, like paper money. Yet for most people the mood was not, strangely perhaps, fear, but a mixture of resignation and simmering excitement; for life was a fast lottery and the day held equal chances of drawing the red instead of the black.

Mexico City was No Man's Land. Generals swept in and out and no one could be sure at any time who was supposed to be sitting in the presidential chair, and most of the time no one was. Villa had his picture taken lolling in it, with Zapata beside him, sitting as if he were made of springs. But the Zapatistas drifted away as they had drifted in, somberly, silently, leaving the townspeople dazed because they had expected a murderous sacking and nothing had happened. When there was no food in the markets the Zapatistas knocked timidly on people's doors and in roundabout gentle Indian style asked for a little something to eat. They were seen in the Palace and the museum walking carefully through the salons, looking at things in each place with curious, respectful interest. Obregón proved to be a much greater terror, for when he occupied the city he levied taxes and issued stringent rulings to sequester food and money, some for the army and some for relief of the famine-stricken poorer population. Severely worded reprimands for his rough handling of business and the clergy were wired from Washington, which Obregón tabled, remarking, "Those gentry seem to believe that it suffices a starving man if you speak to him in a foreign language. . . ."

The decisive military duel developed between Obregón and Villa, with the odds at the start on Villa's side. He and the generals friendly to him held over two-thirds of the country, and outnumbered the Carranza forces perhaps five to one. They had the main railways, quickest access to ammunition, and a friendly press and support of other kinds in the United States. The upper classes and clergy in Mexico preferred Villa too—if they had to choose among bandits. Carranza against this had the oil regions, the best gun-running border territory; and he had, because Obregón was his commander-in-chief, mobile yet unified military methods. Against Villa's massive cavalry attacks, Obregón's strategy was to advance very fast, stop at some good fortifiable point, set up barbed-wire entanglements and lay out trenches, in open-loop shape, in which he put chiefly the Yaqui troops who were the core of his personal army. They had been fighting for generations, trained to win or commit suicide.

When the fight began, the Yaquis lay each one in a trench-hole with his wife and children, who kept handing him a reloaded gun as fast as one was finished; and if he was wounded or killed, they continued firing. Cavalry issued to charge head-on into the Dorados, and then to run apparently routed, into the open loop, where the Yaquis caught the pursuing Dorados in murderous cross-fire. They massacred the first wave, and the second, and sometimes a third. The Dorados, accustomed to being invincible, were not so good at a fourth try, and the same sort of trap closed on them in battle after battle. In short quick pushes Obregón herded Villa northward. The mere fact of retreat began to crumble Villa's army. Its Waterloo was a three-day fight in Celaya, followed by Santa Rosa, in which bloody clash Obregón's right arm was blown off by a grenade. By the middle of 1915 Villa was corralled in the northern deserts, and the United States somewhat dubiously recognized Carranza.

The one essential for winning wars that Villa lacked and Obregón created was political direction. Obregón released the force underneath the struggle for power, and the war swung gradually but with momentum away from fighting simply for loot and excitement, to hammering at the foundations of a better working life. It was because of Obregón that the Carranza headquarters, soon after the convention broke down, issued a decree that said all lands illegally seized by haciendas would be returned. Another decree gave back self-government to the municipalities. A month later Obregón arranged a pact with the Revolutionary Committee of the *Casa del Obrero Mundial* (House of the World Worker), the principal center of organized labor. This agreement, which Carranza swallowed with aversion, committed the Constitutionalist government to support wage and hour laws and the right to organize. In return, the unions would be the allies of the Constitutionalists in the civil war.

The *Casa* moved from Mexico City to military headquarters and got to work very fast. Six "Red Battalions" were organized and thrown into the fighting at once. Units were sent out for construction, repair, espionage, sabotage, and propaganda. One detachment had along a printing press installed in a boxcar, an editorial office which published news and posters and jokes and propaganda, edited by the artist "Dr. Atl" and illustrated by José Clemente Orozco. As each town was taken, the *Casa* opened local quarters there; at the same time as it set up unions, it drew in local industrial labor and harnessed it to the war. Though it was relatively small in numbers, the effect of organization and militant activity snowballed for Carranza. The moral effect of the combination worked in a thousand untraceable ways for the Constitutionalists, since Villa had only his personal legend of bravery and generosity to be fought for.

When Villa was defeated, the pressure to make the promises real at once found Carranza angrily out on a limb. He argued: "Wait till the country is pacified; let's not rock the boat." But this worn argument of those who try to dodge the popular wants that drive revolutions and wars produced the chaos it always does. The struggle became hundreds of separated fights. The Zapatistas continued threatening the capital, while, in the states they dominated, *ejido* and other lands were being taken without benefit of the legal procedures prescribed by Carranza. Throughout the country there were many independent guerrillas unconvinced by Villa's debacle that Carranza was their man. In Carranza territory, labor power was exploding in a mounting series of strikes against paper currency. These things thrust growing bitternesses into the councils of the Carrancistas. There were many political and personal issues, which traced down to the same one: Carranza said the revolution was finished. Obregón, Hill, Alvarado, and other lesser heroes, and a good many of the brain-trusters, big and little, said that the revolution was free now to begin.

Carranza bribed and fenced but his power was draining, and in 1917 he tried to steady his position and put legal bounds around the revolution by calling a Constitutional convention to amend the 1857 charter by which Juárez governed, inserting concessions as of the *status quo*.

It was his intention also to reclaim, by abrogating much Díaz legislation, the original constitutional ideas, which specified lay education and said the subsoil belonged to the nation. The congress met in the city of Querétaro and was attended by the Carranza revolutionary chiefs, their intellectual friends, three or four labor delegates, and a number of deputies and senators of the original Madero congress. The Carranza steering committee was not nearly clever enough, nor strong enough either, to cope with a four-way alliance that included: the military radicals of the north, headed by Obregón; the agrarian-labor generals of the center and south, whose spokesman was the ex-newspaperman General Francisco Mújica; the Zapatista sympathizers, represented by intellectuals; and the labor delegates.

Since this combination stood for a real concentration of army and political power, they had leverage, and turned the assembly into a Constituent Congress that wrote a whole new charter. Its provisions were worked out at top militant speed in committees on which sat a number of men not official delegates, such as Molina Enríquez, who probably wrote most of the agrarian Article 27. Who wrote what else, even those who worked on the job can't trace, except that it was General Mújica who led the parliamentary fight, and Obregón who tooled up and ran the caucus machinery. When they got through they had presented Mexico with the first revolutionary state charter of modern times.

Its theory is: All land and other productive resources belong to the commonwealth, but may be held as private property except when public interest requires otherwise. The subsoil belongs to the nation and may not be owned, but only leased by private parties. The Church may not own property, and foreigners may engage in business only as a Mexican enterprise under the law. Labor is guaranteed the right to organize, the eight-hour day, equal pay for equal work "regardless of sex or nationality," and a detailed list of other advantages and safeguards. *Ejido* and idle lands are to be turned back to the peasants; any landless farmer may petition for a grant if his land has been expropriated, or simply on the basis of need. Education is lay and public and the classic four freedoms of liberal democracy are provided.

Each article that attacks or limits established interests at the same time sets forth protections. The Constitution is thus a Janus document which distills in words the struggles of the congress that wrote it. Perhaps conceived by the philosophers who were present as a bridge from a society based upon capitalism to one based upon socialism, it is so written as to accommodate either capitalism or socialism. Which emphasis is applied depends on who runs the government, and so for twenty-five years Mexico's administrations have been in and out of crises brought on by the fight to apply or not to apply the radical clauses. Yet though the Constitution is a highly mobile thing, it has this character: it can give legal sanction to almost any revolutionary acts that governments may perform, but narrowly limits anti-revolutionary acts. It can move forward or be held still, but can't move back. It expresses in law the concept first articulated clearly in 1917, and since then taken as an axiom: that the civil war was a preface to a continuous social process.

This idea sets the basic pattern of Mexican politics. It is a series of zigzags, traced by the way each administration tackles the same dilemma: on the left, the eighty per cent who want more and more ways produced to make wealth for more and more Mexicans, and who know their power, and know they can use it; on the right, the money, implemented in politics by what Washington wants, and second by the new-rich generals and politicians, and third by the Church, considerably weakened in popular influence but still with a sizable indirect share in business enterprises. This dilemma means a day-to-day conflict for the big generals and politicians who, by inheritance from the revolutionary army, are the group from which important candidates are drawn. The most powerful have become big businessmen, but to stay powerful in politics they must maintain friendly contact with labor and the agrarians, and with the intellectuals who do most of the talking for these two groups. Rich as the generals get, they must remain acceptable as revolutionaries or take a nose-dive when an election year or an economic drag refuels the activities of the have-not-yets. In practice the tugs of war and the juggling produce what look from outside like inscrutable shifts of policy, but it is always the same pattern. Inevitably, the conflict means a very short political life-span for every important politician—maximum, ten years; average, four.

The mechanics of revolutionary politics cut the contemporary story of Mexico sharply into contrasting epochs. Mass pressures and violence as a rule precede and follow each change of administration, and the struggle is always the same, between those who speed and those who brake what Mexicans mean by The Revolution.

When Carranza's term was up in 1919 the revolution's charter—the Constitution of '17—was still mostly rhetoric, a protective covering for a gang of very strange bedfellows. The inflexible Carranza, trying to perform the combined roles of Napoleon and Robespierre; the brilliant-spoken, principled liberal bourgeois Luis Cabrera; the "socialists" from the north and from Yucatán; and the radical ex-students such as Mújica—all were members of this gang, along with a crew of military men who were after two things only, women and money. "The most corrupt administration in Mexico's history," said Calles later, which was certainly cards and spades. Methods were a cross between Díaz and carpetbaggery, and being in the government was still the only profitable business for a Mexican.

There was plenty of public money to dip into, for the World War thirst for oil and the new tax laws were producing a juicy income, though getting it all was hampered by angry argument with the United States (Senator Fall generated and applied the heat) and by less showy action. For a while the oil companies paid and armed a protection man, a guerrilla chief whose job was to keep inspectors off the fields, and fight away the government troops under young General Lázaro Cárdenas. Enough came in, however, to make the chiefs nearest Carranza happy, and to buy in a few of the many others who were still running the revolution as local private enterprise. There was much private enterprise too from within the Carranza fold. *Carranclán*—slang for Carrancista—was the everyday synonym for thief. There was a gray automobile, for instance, that called at night on the houses of the rich, with duly stamped search warrants, and searched the bureau drawers. The searchers were masked, but later somebody recognized a pair of stolen earrings on somebody's mistress, and it turned out that the operators were Carranza's favorite young general and a few gay friends with government jobs.

All the independent chieftains seemed to be getting plenty of arms from somewhere. They kept the small towns in a constant state of alarm and the railroads perpetually crippled. Trains ran only with heavy armed escort. In the north, Villa was playing tag with Pershing's troops. His carefully planned Columbus raid into United States territory in March, 1916, had failed to produce the fall of Carranza by armed intervention. There was an American "invasion" of a sort, but bounded by agreement, stubbornly exacted by Obregón, to stay north of a given line. Mexican government troops camped in the neighborhood, ostensibly to hunt Villa, in reality to attack American detachments straying in the wrong direction. Relations with the United States were a chronic wrangle—the oil taxes, the agrarian laws, the Constitution, the unsettled conditions. Simultaneously there was a Church-government feud. Stories hostile to Mexico permeated the American press. An American cardinal called in New York Mexican Consul Burns to extend an olive branch. He proposed a loan, a large one, "with or without the approval of the United States," if the Con-

stitution provisions affecting the Church were somehow erased. The
money, Consul Burns wrote in his outraged report, was, he thought, a sum
that had been set aside in Germany for Huerta's regime.

In the sugar country, Zapata held out against the government's General
Pablo González, who warred by the "scorched earth" method—he destroyed every village he thought might harbor Zapatistas, killing all the
males. Meanwhile he seemed to be enriching himself by sack, carrying off
hacienda machinery to sell for scrap. He got Zapata finally, through a
junior officer named Guajardo, who put on a good act of wanting to leave
the Federals and join the agrarians, and made it realistic by attacking and
capturing a garrison. When Zapata received him, Guajardo's men lined up
to present arms, and then fired a broadside. The body was slung on the
back of a mule and exhibited in Cuautla, the capital of Morelos, but this
did not convince the agrarians that Zapata was dead. Even now there are
some who say he is alive.

Throughout the rich farming regions, peasants were following Zapatista
doctrines, homesteading regardless of courts and papers, and guarding
the crops with guns. Obregón, not anxious to be the military arm against
the agrarians or any of the revolutionary boys, had retired to "attend to
his own affairs." Hacienda owners willing to risk their lives stayed on
their estates and armed their "good" peasants, who were called White
Guards. So there was always a little war going on around each hacienda,
bloodiest where there was water, most violent at sowing and harvesting
time. The military chief of the region or the governor (usually the same
man) arbitrated thus: Either (1) he made a deal with the owners and
shunted the agrarians off in some unpaid direction; or (2) he made the
fight hotter and bought the place cheap; or (3) he made a deal with the
agrarians to move in and sharecrop with him, but called it a co-operative;
or (4) in a very few cases, he split the land up, leaving the owners the

"small holding" (about six hundred acres) that the agrarian law prescribes, and split the rest among the hacienda workers and nearby villagers. As he got nothing out of this arrangement, it was only the one-in-a-thousand convinced idealist who did it.

When a Mexican government loses its revolutionary virtue, it can continue in power only by force, with external support. The mirage of Germany's strength had flickered out with the end of the World War. Carranza made his peace offering. He put forth to succeed him in the presidency the classic candidate of appeasement—Mexico's Ambassador to Washington, an inoffensive diplomat named Bonillas. The boys made short shrift of that project. They mustered around Obregón; and Carranza, trying to force a decision, went so far as to have Obregón arrested, charged with "plotting sedition." He escaped and, with troops reinforced by agrarians, advanced on the capital.

There were no troops to send willingly against Obregón. Carranza gathered up the government and put it in special trains which carried all the more precious contents of the National Palace and the Treasury, shoveled in sacks and loaded in boxcars, with the Ministers wedged in among the valuables. What troops he had were aboard the rear trains. Before he started for Veracruz, Carranza wired Guadalupe Sánchez, in command of that region (one of his favored generals), and got this reply: "President and father, though everyone else betray you, I shall not. If but one man remain loyal to you, I am that man." Sánchez then marched his eight thousand boys to intercept the trains.

Some railroaders loosed a "wild locomotive" from behind as the convoy groaned through the rim of the Valley of Mexico, wrecking the munitions cars and cutting off retreat. Halfway down the plateau, Sánchez' boys attacked. For several days the convoy inched through the mountains, fighting. It was finally sandwiched at Rinconada, where attackers from the rear caught up. While the victorious Obregonistas were taking inventory of the properties disgorged by the wrecked convoy, Carranza and a few aides pushed their sweated horses up wild trails into Indian country. The third night, Carranza slept in a mudfloored hut in a place called Tlaxcalantongo, and was killed. Instead of the mourning ballads sung in the markets when men die who are loved by many, Carranza's tragedy was jingled:

> Now's the time old beard-tenango
> You must get smart-monkey-chango
> For off in Tlaxcalantongo
> They've cut out your gizzard-ongo.

Mexico for the Mexicans

THERE WAS A LIFT, a stirring feel in Mexico in the early '20's, when the last chief had made his arrangements with Obregón, and each agrarian cradled his gun in some safe place, like the roof thatch. It was new, it was a spring world where fear was skewered.

Young people saw their lives ahead through open doors. There was a sense of strength released: much work to do, everything at the beginning, leeway for anyone to make his way as independently in peace as in guerrilla fighting. There would be room for all to be useful with dignity, learn, build, be free. The inequalities, the injustices, the helpless poverties of the past could now no longer be accepted; they would be destroyed irreverently. Poets wrote lyrics about high-tension cables. Peasants hung necklaces of flowers on tractors and invented Indian nicknames for steam shovels. Songs like this nursed the hush of the village evenings:

Pancho Villa has surrendered
In the city of Torreón,
He is tired now of fighting
And now cotton will be grown.

Now we are all one party,
There is no one left to fight;
The war is ended, *compañeros*,
Let us work, it is our right.

I would like to be a great man
With much wisdom in my head,
But I would much rather have
Every day my daily bread.

Now the cornfields are in tassel,
The kernels are tight on the ear;
It's the sustenance of man—
The holiest thing that there is.

Villa with his two hundred last guerrillas had settled for a big ranch in the north, and was happily absorbed in the wonders of agricultural machinery and scientific cattle-breeding. Elsewhere, in many spots, other chiefs had chucked their uniforms and were embracing mechanization and struggling through pages on crop improvement and pest control, expecting with fierce pride to make the land bear as it had never borne before. There was a knot of such new landholders in every zone in Mexico. Numerically small but politically potent, they pushed to open roads, raised dams, cut channels, sunk wells, celebrating each fresh cascade and reservoir and hovering over the arrival of majestic Brahma bulls and rangy longhorns. The mountain hollows that had served them so well as hide-outs were turned to pasture for lambs and fuzzy calves and pleased, jingling young goats. At Chapingo, near Mexico City, a rich hacienda that had belonged to Díaz' playboy friend, General Manuel González, became an agricultural college.

The cabins where peons had been chained at dark remained as museum pieces, but the pool built for the general's harem, fabulous as Solomon's, was cleaned and refilled for the brown-faced boys. The hungering dream of land to cultivate each for himself was coming true, every Mexican would have his tinted house, his field and orchard, his chickens and geranium pots. The chiefs, big and lesser, were appeased and many saw to it that their soldiers got fertile patches too. No one disputed that room must be made for all. The country would grow rich and strong, made so by the people, for the people . . .

Obregón, with his paternal smile, distributed the power in a manner that has been followed by every administration since. Two or three of the profitable ministries and top posts were reserved to generals, who passed the work along to agile brain-trusters. The rest of the cabinet (Obregón believed that active military should not participate in government) was made up of civilians who were either honest economists or technicians themselves or in any case men of culture with imagination enough to go along with the brain-trusters. The revolutionary chiefs, taking their cue from Obregón, were eager to pay for their power (and the fat rewards thereof) with revolutionary works. Even those who were mere robber barons were as sincere participants in the new credos as the crusader knights who devoutly portioned their Moorish loot with the Church. So any man who had a good idea and who got it listened to by a general or an important politician had the chance to try it out, or made the chance himself. Ideas in progress ranged from irrigation plans to free breakfasts in the schools to serum laboratories and baby clinics and wall newspapers and beggars' hostels and art for the people and cheap editions of Plutarch. Some of the libraries, clinics, and shelters were housed (with enthusiastic symbolism) in nationalized churches.

Artists returning from guerrilla trooping and from war-exhausted Europe organized a "Syndicate of Painters, Sculptors, and Intellectual Workers," headed beamingly by Diego Rivera, some of whose Parisian friends were now high in new Soviet councils. The painters got contracts for murals, at plasterer's rates, from the Minister of Education, and swaggered in overalls up splintery scaffolds to put the meaning of the revolution, thrice human size, on public walls. What they painted was like nothing any of them had done before. They had something to say that they felt deeply and wanted to communicate with force. Foreign critics saw the work in progress and said with awe that this was the first great modern art created in America, but the best people screamed in the press and their pious sons ganged up to scratch the walls at night and throw corrosives on the monumental figures. The painters took that gleefully as a tribute, and came to work with pistols in their pockets. The great Indian faces and the overpowering compositions, linked deliberately to ancient Mexican art and to Italian primitives, taught this religion: beauty is all that is native, active, living, earthly, all that is productive work. They said *Mexico for all the Mexicans . . . is socialism* as clearly as Cimabue said *Christianity,* and Rivera's were reinforced with painted words from revolutionary songs and current poems: "The land belongs to him who works it" . . . and:

> Comrade miner
> Bowed by the weight of the earth
> When your hands take out the metals
> Fashion daggers.
> Then you will know
> That all the metals are for you.

In the slums of Mexico City a shabby young man named Miguel Oropeza piled a wheelbarrow with books and went from door to door offering to lend them free; and the inhabitants, folk with the reputation of apaches, found themselves with him helping their small boys and girls to build their own adobe school; which the children ran, the classes being "co-operative

unions" taught by the eldest, or by whichever child knew something—
reading, figuring, how to make bread or plant squashes. In another poor
section Dr. Mariano Azuela put away his Texan hat and fighting outfit
and opened a clinic, writing (between working hours) the revolutionary
novels that made him famous . . . while he continued quietly to run his
clinic and see the same distressed kind of patients. Out in Teotihuacán
Dr. Manuel Gamio, a scholar who had studied anthropology at Columbia,
with Boas, made himself a double-barreled job. He was at the same time
digging the great ruined pyramids and temples and trying to uncover what
was in the minds of living *teotihuacanos*. His eloquent book *Forjando
patria* (Welding a Country) said that Indians and mestizos were the base
of the modern society Mexico could build strongly; and to do this teachers
should first learn, like missionaries, and be guided by what those they
would teach wanted to know, and thought most interesting, and needed
for their immediate practical benefit.

The Department of Education, housed in a reconditioned convent and
filled with the scaffolds of the mural painters, was the forum of most of
the human-interest projects all to be done at once in a hurry. It was a headquarters busy with the tack-tack-crash of typewriters, with stenographers
dressed as if for a fiesta, with sandaled delegations to see the rural-schools
department or maybe just the murals, with idea-traders and saviors and
philosophers and students and foreigners arguing about the paintings.

Some of the visitors were political exiles from Central and South American countries, who were given asylum and welcome and jobs, with no
distinctions made between them and Mexicans. When they went home,
often to positions of prestige and power, they taught and applied the
meaning of the Mexican Revolution; and throughout the continent uneasy
stirrings warned the beneficiaries of each "Porfirian Peace" of avalanches
coming. A few of the visitors to the Department of Education were Krem-
lin delegates, with revolutionary greetings, who often settled down with

teaching jobs and lives rooted in Mexico. The University absorbed one or two who have taught the present generation of brain-trusters socialist economics and have continued as professors long after they broke with the Stalin-era party.

From the Department of Education issued hundreds of young people on absurdly low salaries, rural schoolteachers called missionaries, which word described precisely their state of mind and the hardship of their jobs. They had first to persuade the villagers (sometimes in Aztec or another Indian language) that they came to take nothing, and next they had to help them get a school of some sort built, with perhaps a hut or shack for the teacher to live in. Their classes included, with abc and 1-2-3, rudimentary sanitation, rudimentary pest control and crop rotation, the significance of the revolution, and the practice of sports. And as these schools began to breach the heretofore undisputed mental authority of the priests, the jobs not infrequently ended in mutilation and massacre at the hands of exalted fanatics told thus to save their souls.

In the Department of Agriculture Ramón de Negri, a man whom no hacienda owner found sympathetic, wrestled with the geography of the agrarian problem. Minus a thousand and one complexities, here is what the problem is made of. More than three-fourths of the population are accustomed to live by farming. But half the country's surface is mountain. Of the other half, only fourteen per cent has water, for the rains drain as they fall, from the high plateau to the coasts. Of this fourteen per cent, only half of the crop lands are sown each year and the rest are let lie fallow. Thus fifteen million people (nineteen now) had to be fed from the crops of seventeen and a half million acres, almost all farmed in primitive ways.

The agrarian law said that each family head or young farmer was entitled to ask for a parcel of his own, ranging in size from seven acres of

humid land to twenty acres of dry-farm land. The average, then, would
be fourteen acres. There were three million plus, rural families, of whom
over ninety per cent were landless. Of the total thirty-five million acres of
crop lands, over four-fifths were haciendas. The acreage that could be
classified as *ejido* land, idle land, other expropriable land, came, plus public lands, to no more than ten per cent of this. If the haciendas were re-
spected except for the nibblings the law suggested, there were three and a
half million acres to satisfy the three million family heads and others who
were entitled to ask for fourteen-acre parcels each. Even over-all expropriation would not be enough, if the land were divided individually, and
it was argued by Obregón that the country's economy and tax-budget could
not stand the jolt. Well—let irrigation—industrialization—future administrations—take care of the tragic discrepancy. The Department of Agriculture could start making available what there was.

Spectacled men in riding pants, with instruments and papers strapped
in cases, arrived at spots where the local war between *hacendados* and
landless was noisiest and bloodiest. They surveyed, measured, listened,
spread out their maps on tables around which sat like images the village
elders or the "agrarian committee." In Morelos the committee members
were almost invariably scarred Zapatistas. Elsewhere they might be purely
village-chosen, or mixed with one or two men close to some local politician, a state deputy perhaps, perhaps a governor's henchman. The committee, dressed usually in peasant white, barefoot or sandaled, weighed
every line and wiggle on the maps with great deliberation, suggesting
changes—a little more water here, a little less of the eroded slope over
there.

The land would be held by individual title, as the agrarian law prescribed, but might be worked either in common or partly individually and
partly in common, according to the ancient Indian usage still familiar to
most villages. When the day arrived, the distribution was a solemn ritual.

The peasants gazed at the blueprints long and incredulously, letting happiness show only in their eyes. They went through the proceedings with religious dignity, celebrating as on saints' holiest days, with firecrackers at regular intervals. The agrarian engineer, officiating, took on the aura of respect up to now reserved for priests. And as more and more peasants grew to know the word *ingeniero* (engineer) in terms of distributions, irrigation projects, crop knowledge, pest control, their distrust receded and they said it deferentially, like a title of honor.

The *hacendados* fought back, trying government channels and sometimes succeeding, and increasing their ammunition dumps and, if they could, the size of their "good peasant" White Guards (who melted away as the chance of an engineer's final visit might increase). A few fought physically, for themselves. Mrs. Rosalie Evans, a British woman to whom the revolutionary surge looked, quite naturally, like nothing but banditry unleashed, refused to permit the portions of her hacienda claimed by agrarian villagers to be removed. She appealed to the generals, to the governor, to Obregón, to the American press, to the American Embassy, and the British minister fumed and rumbled. To all this Obregón pleasantly, with increasing firmness, said: "Observe the law." Mrs. Evans went back to her hacienda and herself, with guns and helpers and a pack of dogs, attacked the ploughers and harvesters on the claims, and, parapeted on the roof, held her manor against counterattacks. She was killed in ambush. And her blind angry pitiful letters were published, adding international pressure to the agrarian problem; which was accumulating nationally, for everywhere peasants were sending delegations to the capital to present their claims to the government engineers. In many ticklish cases all they wanted was to "revalidate" claims that were already being worked, with arms cached in the bushes and a lookout on top of the hill. The committees often now were in touch with each other, and in many zones there were strong Agrarian Leagues, of great political weight. In Yucatán the governor, Felipe Carrillo Puerto, a gentle-voiced and unobtrusive man, set them up himself, naming them "Leagues of Resistance" (to resist the henequen planters). The inaugural act was to read the Constitution, slowly and in good Maya that any peasant could understand. Another gubernatorial figure, Emilio Portes Gil, was seeing to it that agrarians and unions were organized in his oil state of Tamaulipas. In every state and zone there was somebody, a governor or a deputy or a senator, or many somebodies, mobilizing organized power. Village delegations to the capital multiplied and kept coming, and coming back, month after month, tenacious as life itself; filling the ministerial waiting rooms with ceremonious Indian murmurs.

In the Treasury, Adolfo de la Huerta struggled with the arithmetic of the same kind of problem, trying to stretch by scrupulous bookkeeping what there was toward what was needed. This was still the time when gushers of the Golden Lane were in fabulous production, and the tax income from oil and other sources had been climbing by as much as a third to a half each year. But, for example, clean drinking water for every community that needed it would cost, even disregarding the "bites" all down the line, more than three times the total annual government income. Moreover, there were very few possible sources of taxes. The haciendas had been operating haphazardly for so long that most of them were mortgaged to the hilt, and they could not take much of a load without bankruptcy, while, if they were cut up, new owners starting from scratch would have to have financial backing, tax concessions, machinery—all representing outlay rather than income for some years ahead. The customs were pledged, by old agreements, in great proportion to service the foreign debt. The few industries—mines, oil, textiles—were foreign-owned, and every tax move in that direction meant an acute international problem, with jeopardy. The only sources of finance were external, and to secure money there the Obregón government had to get recognized, and, to get recognized, it would have to acknowledge and service the debt, and also pay a costly bill for damages and losses caused to foreigners by the revolution.

In the Foreign Affairs Department the problem was the same as in all the others—strategy from the short end of the Golden Rule. Albert B. Fall, United States Secretary of the Interior, was the Mexican expert in the Harding Administration. He served upon Obregón a formidable list of demands that required a return to Díaz conditions, with extras. Obregón answered truthfully that he had not the power to make such concessions; the answer was warships in the Tampico neighborhood.

For a time it looked as if the old formula—Move In, Take It Over, Save Mexico from Herself—were going to be employed. But an American mining man and banker, John B. Glenn, who had been a consular agent and had seen the revolution at close quarters, and had been around with Obregón and other chiefs, knew what that would mean. The revolution, he was convinced, was inevitable and necessary, and Obregón he thought was a fine man doing a fine job. He managed to persuade the oil men and bankers in New York to get down to Mexico and talk things over. This led to a series of semi-official, extremely secret conversations in a private house on Bucareli Street. The two Harding envoys wanted the Constitution suspended as it applied to oil, and to labor in foreign concerns; they also wanted the agrarian law to apply only to Mexican owners; they wanted the crippled railroads fixed and returned to the old management, and the debt serviced, and the damages . . .

Obregón, a subtle, experienced practitioner of the Mexican defensive art of saying "yes, tomorrow," or just elaborately "yes" (with apologies later for the unfortunate circumstances that prevented fulfillment) said yes to a little of everything. The "Bucareli Conference" ended with an understanding that the Americans thought was a treaty and that the Mexicans said was a gentleman's agreement, unofficially Obregón's. The impression was that the Constitution would not be applied "retroactively," that is, that the oil in deposits being worked, or already in concession, would not be claimed by the State. Labor would be made, in roundabout ways, to behave itself; while in return the Americans would scale down the debt and would look the other way as regards land distribution. The railroads would remain in government hands. All claims for damage and loss would be handled by a mixed commission and the government would pay a portion . . . eventually. It proposed also to give agrarian bonds to expropriated landholders, Americans and other foreigners and Mexicans alike, which would be redeemed . . . when the government had the money.

The Obregón government was then conceded to be in existence and one of the Harding negotiators, Charles Beecher Warren, was made the Coolidge ambassador; and was soon replaced by another steward of American life and property, James R. Sheffield. De la Huerta went up to New York to get a loan with which to start a government bank. He sweated and writhed, caught between the upper millstone of what the bankers wanted and the nether millstone of what Obregón and the Mexican Congress would not agree to. He went home with a "Lamont–De la Huerta Agreement" that raised the wind in Congress and cost him his Cabinet post and wrecked his career.

Money to make the revolution solvent was not obtainable except on the promise of unmaking the revolution. But an idea glimmered through, and this idea turned out to be the first break in Mexico's dilemma. Get money where bankers get it—in banking. And where businessmen get it —in business. Glenn gave Obregón some shrewd assistance and the new Secretary of the Treasury, Alberto Pani, was a nimble, unconventional financier. The orthodox practice, tax and spend to govern, was steered into tax and spend to produce and collect a profit. First, the government made itself the sole silver exporter, reaping the commissions and profits and establishing a critically needed balance of dollars in the United States. The same idea was applied to other major exports, as for instance henequen, which was marketed by a producers' pool through government intervention. Next, a national bank was set up, with government and private banking funds—or else. This eased the wild currency zigzags to some extent and step by step the government bank got the dominant position in national finance, along lines comparable to the Federal Reserve and the (later) RFC, but run from a sharply different point of view. Some of the foreign banks withdrew, others stayed with limited operations.

These measures brought startling economic changes. Hardly by plan, but in reaction to urgent pressures, administrations that followed branched the banking (much of the time under the direction of Pani and others still more unconventional) into provincial banks set up especially to give credit to the new and smaller farmers. And further branched into many other kinds of credit institutions and funds: co-operative credit unions, mortgage, housing, insurance, manufacturing combinations. In twenty years, though most business and industry is still private, the government has become the biggest single operator. Few of the enterprises which it backs are completely government-owned and run. Instead there are many different kinds of combinations; in some the government is simply the banker, in others it is an active partner, and there is a great variety of set-ups in between.

The government's position as banker, exporter, buyer, marketer, importer, producer, and promoter, with all the ramifications of these activities, gave it ultimate power over production and prices, but without particular institutions or bureaus or laws set up for that purpose. This power has been exercised in somewhat the same manner as the RFC, the Export-Import Bank, and other United States government institutions such as the Surplus Commodities Corporation, but in exactly opposite directions. In the United States, until war came, the effort of the New Dealers was to raise prices, diminish the production of farm staples, and in general sustain industry without expanding it. The opposite policies, which we discovered necessary when war came, have operated in Mexico. Price control has generally been control downward; production control, upward pump-priming, to the neediest enterprises; financing, to the smallest; public-works spending, on necessities, never on "made work." The idea has been to make and back and multiply independent enterprise, Mexican owned and run, and preferably for national consumption.

The effect has been a great release of productive power, and a subtle change of attitude, a growth of individual dignity and independence; for a government job or politics are no longer the only security and profit to be sought by young people finishing school. The production index has been a kind of terraced pyramid upward, rising steeply soon after each time the administration changed hands from those who had prospered to those who had not yet done so. Its by-products: a fast-increasing government income from diversified sources; a new middle class, moneymakers with government footholds of the type we have long known well; a consumer-goods industry; cheap money accompanied by rising prices; a higher wage level; and a greatly enlarged industrial proletariat. In the cities, a perceptible spread of goods and comforts. And because of roads and a little newly created peasant credit, a sediment in the villages of something remotely resembling the chance of prosperity.

That is the economic story of the years after the civil war. A part of the nation, perhaps five per cent, is very prosperous; another ten or fifteen per cent earns comfortably; another fifteen or twenty per cent, while very poor by our standards, has much, much more than in the Díaz days. The rest has more, but is still close to the coolie level. The distance between the haves and the have-not-yets is still appalling, and since the revolution changed apathy to appetite, the civil war continues in political form.

The government remains fundamentally a military dictatorship, as it has been from the beginning of the Mexican Republic. The traditional heir-apparent to the presidential chair is still the ranking military hero, who is always the potential leader of revolt. But since the revolution he also needs to be, like Obregón, a man of advanced political ideas, or at least a skilful appeaser of labor and the agrarians. However right-wing his intentions, he must appear continuously left. The military can no longer hold the power, or even obtain it, relying only on themselves. They have to have the active support and sometimes the armed assistance of the peasants and organized labor. They need as go-betweens, and to administer the government, a corps of brain-trusters—steadily increasing in number as time goes on—who are propagandists, technicians, and intellectuals of extremely advanced ideas. They are the real policy-makers, within the limits set up by the power and cash ambitions of the limelighted *políticos.*

The machine for climbing no longer consists of piety and high connections and police talents. Politicians on the make now try to organize or strengthen unions, co-operative leagues, agrarian leagues, labor federations, whose leaders, though grinding one or another political axe, cannot guarantee their boys. Such organizations—labor in its widest application and including some professions—are channels through which popular pressure reaches, with effect, to those who govern. So they have worked out to be the first rudimentary instruments of workable democracy. The ruling politicos have tried from time to time to subordinate them in a "monolithic national party," which includes spokesmen from these organizations, and intellectuals, and all the rest of the "revolutionary family." The civil war transfers then to the inner-party councils and the party seldom lasts beyond two administrations. Presenting itself as all things to all men, it wears its promise out and has to be revamped and tinkered up and given new names.

Almost necessarily, high office is filled from the ranks of the military, for the generals are the "boys in the back room." Now they are also the biggest Mexican industrialists, businessmen, ranchers, and farmers. This sooner or later brings them into conflict with labor, and they try to dodge the issue sometimes by uttering radical sentiments and backing reform laws, and sometimes by steering the lightning elsewhere—to the Church, or preferably to American or other foreign capital, still the really big money. And this of course produces heat from Washington, and brings the revolution out into the open again. To the degree that Mexico-United States relations grow warmly cordial, most Mexicans become uneasiest. They often quote what some one of them said long ago: "God preserve us from the friendship of the United States!"

There are three doctrines: complete socialization, middle ground through co-operatives, and capitalist organization. The cycle of official doctrine goes from the first to the third, depending on which set of pressures—those from Washington or those exerted by the unappeased eighty per cent—is most immediately ominous. Politicians shift to meet each pressure, and when the pressure becomes a danger, administrations shift—or appear to. There is a recurring pattern, often marked at the shifting point with explosive violence. Administrations with strong left-wing direction give way to "pacifiers," and these in turn usher in business booms, appease foreign capital, and are then, as a rule, ousted by threatened revolt. Each time the lefts come in again they are more sharply radical.

The political story of the two decades since Obregón zigzags according to these conflicts. The lurid events of those years, the news now, the stir tomorrow, connect like the plot of a play within these combinations, which are the "dynamics" of Mexican politics. The individual characters, being human, are hardly so predictable.

To follow Obregón in 1924 there was no one who could match his military record and political resource, nor above all who had the liking and respect of so many different kinds of people. The nearest likeness was his old friend and campaign partner General Benjamín Hill, who was Minister of War in the Obregón Cabinet and therefore automatically the first likely choice. He died suddenly, believed poisoned. Then Villa (who might again harbor a yen for the chair that an Indian wit once said would insure peace if it were a bench) died suddenly too. He was ambushed by a hired killer on the way to his ranch. These prefaces to the elections were interpreted in malicious gags to signify that Plutarco Elías Calles meant to be president.

His only serious challenger was Adolfo de la Huerta, popular with middle-class and business groups, and well connected with labor. He had been made provisional president when Carranza was killed, to hold the chair until Obregón was duly installed by election, and had then taken over the Treasury. It was understood there was a deal, by which he would follow Obregón, in regular tenure, and Calles was to come next. But Calles after all was a general, and he had an ace up his sleeve in the form of a written contract with the soft-spoken, strong-arm labor czar, Luis Morones. A barrage of publicity was played upon De la Huerta's Treasury record and further doubt was cast on his revolutionary calibre by the fact that Catholic politicians favored him.

Obregón hesitated, then threw his support to Calles, who was elected in due course, and made a trip to the United States, where he was dined by Secretary Hughes and banqueted in New York, and was inaugurated December 1, 1924. De la Huerta raised the customary "Imposition!" and made the customary move, revolt. He was supported by a strong list of unsatisfied generals, with troops and supplies, and by some left-wing labor groups. Further backing came from propertied folk who feared that Calles would be even more radical than Obregón. Civil war broke out again, with particular ferocity in the rich hacienda states. Carrillo Puerto was stood against a wall and shot, with members of his family. Obregón called on the *agrarista* peasants for help. They came silently in crowds, some bringing their own guns. Even so, the fighting went on for months. It was ended when Obregón flanked De la Huerta by swinging troops over the border and around, through U. S. territory, with permission of the Coolidge government. (De la Huerta fled to Los Angeles and there earned his living as a singing teacher; years afterwards, when Cárdenas invited all political exiles to return, he came back and was given a job as inspector in the Consular Service.)

American papers ran hopeful editorials, pegged to the speech Calles had made in October 1924 at the Waldorf-Astoria: his policy would be to raise, economically and socially, "the submerged twelve million," but at the same time to invite the co-operation of capitalists and industrialists of good will. The revolution was over. Meanwhile in Mexico Calles declared that the sacrifices made to put down the counter-revolution would not be in vain. He was a socialist, he announced, and his would be a labor government. He was a man of the people. Hadn't he been a poor country school-teacher when he joined the Madero movement? (There were no reminders that he had been a bartender also, and a tough one.) The big slogan was "honest government" and an imposing show was made of carrying it out. The net was a cleanup mainly affecting Obregón's boys, which made room for a new power machine. The miserable salaries of government employees (springboard of graft) remained miserable.

Luis Morones, boss of the CROM, the national labor federation, had once been an electrician and was now the kind of union leader who in the United States makes at least $25,000 a year. He had coupled the unions of the CROM (*Confederación Regional Obrera Mexicana*) to a tight political party set up for the purpose of making Calles president. In return, Calles had contracted to clear all rails for the CROM and to make Morones the head of a new Ministry of Labor and Industry. Activity receded from the Department of Agriculture and the focus shifted to this new building. Morones had three jobs: cabinet minister, head of the national

munitions factory, and leader of the CROM. His positions gave him decisive power to roll up CROM membership, to enforce the closed shop in
CROM plants, and to cripple unions outside the CROM. He had many
advantages, for he had the last word in strike decisions, which had to be
submitted to the labor-employer arbitration boards under his jurisdiction.

The inner council of the CROM was a semi-secret society, about a dozen
men, called the *Grupo Acción*. They not only ran the CROM but also
pooled and swapped to get or control the key posts in the government—
avoiding, of course, any trespass on the Ministry of War. And there was
a still more secret society of quiet fellows with steel persuaders who saw
to it that Morones' will was done. The CROM treasury was kept more
than full, not from dues (which most of the members couldn't afford or
didn't pay), but through political patronage, kickbacks, and such devices.
Morones spent like a rajah, and not from the CROM treasury. Why should
he, with the National Treasury available?

CROM members got real benefits, of course, from their organization:
upped wages, improved working conditions, compensation laws, and supreme bargaining power. Still, they were not very enthusiastic over the
spectacle of Morones, who came to look like the cartoons of the Bloated
Plutocrat. Monstrously fat, sparkling with diamonds, he rode with his
bodyguards in lustrous cars, to and from his cozy hideouts in the suburbs.
He was a sight even less edifying to the *agrarista* peasants, for from
Morones' viewpoint the less land distributed, the more land workers there
were to be organized in unions or leagues from the CROM. The new
government doctrine as regards land distribution was that, since the acreage
expropriable strictly within the letter of the flexible and complex law was
obviously insufficient, the left-over millions of landless should consider
themselves hacienda labor, and should choose to better their condition by
the same recourses as industrial labor.

Landholders could allow for the small portions claimable by law, and

relax. All property titles were secure. The nation would be built safely on
the base of the small farmers and businessmen (in which definition Calles
& Company included themselves) who would be multiplied by government help. To that end, government-in-business and business-in-government now clearly emerged. The national bank, astutely managed by
Calles' smart economic advisers, took its dominant position in finance; the
agricultural banks were started, and where individual farmers were too
small or weak to be good credit risks, they were pulled together into co-
operative credit unions and pools. More money was appropriated for more
dams and roads, planned and built entirely, and pointedly, by Mexicans.
The first great highways were chopped and blasted through the sierras to
connect the coasts, and toward the United States. And the Indians living
on those heights, in an archaic world, looked at the twentieth century as
at a set of remarkable toys. In one road camp a construction foreman
rigged up a belt and hitched his car motor to a corn-grinder; the women,
who lived and died bending several hours daily over a grinding-stone,
stared, some with tears in their eyes.

The capital took on the Coolidge-era outlook. Factories were being
started and growing, stores installed big plate glass windows, electric ad-
vertising signs flashed up, American trade names became as well known
as the names of movie stars. Calles' secretary opened a chain of popsicle
stands. A construction company owned by Calles' friends was paving the
streets. There was hot trade in many kinds of contracts and concessions.
A government economist sardonically commented: "The style has changed;
it used to be simple graft, Spanish system, which leaves nothing; now it
is constructive graft, American system, which builds everything." The
roistering old-style generals metamorphosed into something more suitable
for country clubs and Rotary. General Joaquín Amaro removed his earrings, had himself taught good English, and added polo etiquette to his
magnificent mustang horsemanship. There was a boom in Mexico City

and resort real estate. In Cuernavaca, where once Carlotta and Maximilian had wandered in romantic gardens, there sprang up a row of mansions inhabited by the new tycoons. It was nicknamed Ali Baba Street.

Calles & Co., like the chiefs of the Obregón days, had also to do revolutionary works as showily as possible, for the burden of proof was weighing more heavily as the land program slowed down and the number of cars, houses, plants, haciendas, and women kept by the leading *políticos* grew blatant. They did all they could that wouldn't disturb their properties or enrage Washington. The budget for education was increased. Schools were built by the hundred. The National Department of Health took several steps into the morass of disease submerging all but the very rich. Milk, at least in the cities (where it could be bought), now got some sort of inspection. Smallpox epidemics, at least in the larger towns, were curbed by vaccination. A Pasteur Institute made rabies serum, for whoever could get to the capital in time to take it. Posters described some symptoms and consequences of syphilis, explained the brutifying effects of intestinal parasites, dramatized the disasters of alcoholism. These were often put up on school walls and the Association of Catholic Parents began a special campaign in alarm, saying the public school system was given over to immorality; stories of wild debauchery were circulated warning parents against the atheistic government schools, where boys and girls—imagine!—were actually taught in the same room.

The dams, roads, schools, hospitals, banks, contracts, and extras, not to mention at least repairing the battered railroads, called for money, and more money. Though the Treasury's income rose steadily from the great increase of production and new taxes, regularly collected, it was still absurdly small against all the things that had to be done, all dangerously urgent. Maybe . . . well . . . there were the oil fields, still producing the easiest big money in Mexico, and paying proportionately very low taxes. The Constitution was still bereft of the enabling legislation by which its radical articles, oil, labor, Church, land, could be applied. Congress picked up the document and drove into the job, in a storm of arguments and shouts and catcalls and drawing of guns. One prominent senator who was bucking Morones was waylaid and murdered.

This game was for big stakes. The lawmakers were taut with excitement and each clause, each comma almost, was fought through. And what was coming through produced angry surprise in Washington, where there was already some displeasure because Nicaraguans resisting U. S. Marines were getting help from Mexico. Secretary Kellogg harangued and scolded and said that the American government, though it favored stability and orderly constitutional procedure, would continue to support the Mexican government only so long as it complied with its international obligations by protection of American lives and rights in Mexico. It was, he said, a disorderly Bolshevist country and was "on trial before the world." The answers were elaborately dignified. It wasn't "customary for governments to argue about one another's internal legislation, and highly irregular to complain about laws still in the process of being written."

While this dogfight was going on, by a coincidence frequently observed in Mexican politics, the Church conflict broke into the open too. The Constitution, like every Mexican constitution since the country had freed itself of the Spanish crown, was not acceptable to the Church. Whoever swore allegiance to that first charter was excommunicated; and, as every charter since had mined more deeply under the Church's once total power, they were all, in its eyes, documents of the devil. This one, which left the Church nothing but the right to function as a religion, and which moreover limited its number of clergy, and required them to be Mexicans, was . . . not to be tolerated. An oblique campaign had been going on to teach that government should be by-passed because Christ is King. There had been solemn ceremonies of coronation, some outdoors on symbolic hilltops, despite the sixty-year-old law confining religious ceremonies to church

premises. Now, while the tempest growled in the north, the Church declared that it would not submit to the Constitution as it applied to the
clergy. Instead it would go on strike. Rather than register, priests would
cease to officiate altogether; and all good Catholics were urged to carry
on a boycott of purchasing in order to paralyze national economy.

In this test of strength, Masses became a bootleg article, carried on at
risk of a government raid. Priests behaved and were treated like outlaws.
In Jalisco the bishop led armed rebels; and in the capital Calles, with
screaming publicity, sent one well-known priest to the firing squad. Boys
and girls of fine family met with nuns and clerical leaders to make and
spread propaganda, some in print and some in bombs. Guerrillas called
cristeros (Christers) raided the rural schools and left the bodies of teachers labeled with banners and placards reading "Christ is King."

The Calles government made the most out of the two conflicts. "Here,"
said its spokesmen with a pointing finger, "are the enemies. Here are the
forces in league—the oil companies, the gringos, and the Church. They are
the exploiters. This is why the Mexican people are still penniless in one
of the richest lands in the world."

And in Washington, mouthpieces for Doheny, and Standard Oil, and
what was left of the Teapot Dome boys, and Hearst cried for intervention,
while the Knights of Columbus raised a million dollars to help the Christ-
the-King guerrillas. But the people of the United States were weary of
violent imperialisms, so Congress didn't warm to expeditionary projects.
Instead, President Coolidge sent Dwight Morrow in the fall of 1927 to
try sweet reason on the debt, the oil, the Church, the land, and the labor
problems.

The dramas in scarehead, the riots round the churches, all provided a
sense of national jeopardy, but there was no rally to Calles. Nobody saw
much of a Moses in his iron face. Nor was there any national rush to support the Church. The majority feeling was skeptical, sullen, or aloof, as

if the fights were contests for championships that had nothing to do with private folk. Most of the priests were sheltered in rich houses, where the family was pretty actively in the fight. In the little places, the parish appointed a committee to look after the church and perform services, after their fashion. The main thing was that the images should not be harmed. A few country priests, almost pure Indian and poor, without connections in the cities or influence at the See, stayed where they were and were hidden in caves and gullies when the need arose. Later, when the fight was over and those who had gone began coming back, they were not well received in many villages; some would not take them back at all, saying they could not afford it. Few peasants, except White Guards at the haciendas, joined the *cristeros*, though the Church had counted heavily on the piety of the eighty per cent. But the priests had been preaching that to be an agrarian was a great sin. Well, said the peasants, the kingdom of heaven is their concern but what we want is a taste of the kingdom of earth.

It was obvious as the Calles term ran out that no Callista could get the presidential seat and remain in it very long. The only man with enough prestige and popular backing and a suave hand for trouble was Obregón, but he was barred by law, the Madero slogan that ends all official communications: "Effective Suffrage, No Re-election." An emergency decree was quickly set up by Congress providing technicalities by which he could sit again, and the elections went through according to plan.

Ten days before Obregón's inaugural in July, 1928, all the key men of the *gran familia revolucionaria* gathered in a hall in the flowery suburb of San Ángel, to banquet the chief. A seedy young man drifted in, making caricatures of the banqueters. Nobody paid attention. Art on the spot is often peddled like songs and lottery tickets in eating and drinking places. The drawings were passed around, they were handed up to the place of honor, and the young man hovered about. He nudged in, slipped his hand into his shoddy black coat, and fired. Obregón pitched over, dying.

The public learned, from a trial that filled the front pages for many days, that the killer's name was León Toral and that he was a member of a terrorist group that had decided that Christ the King required the sacrifice of someone's life in exchange for Obregón's. A nun and a zealot, the leaders of the group, were banished to a prison island off the Pacific coast, where, some time later, they were married. Toral was executed, and believers waited for miracles to be performed by scraps of the killer's personal belongings.

Peace of a sort was engineered by the provisional president, close-mouthed Emilio Portes Gil, a civilian revolutionary from the north with an Indian face and Indian gift for subtle politics; he had been governor of Tamaulipas and Secretary of the Interior, stepping from there to the provisional presidency as the law establishes. He was not thought a Callista, for he was identified with the agrarian wing of the party and with anti-CROM unions. He ran the government for two years with Calles' backing. The public thought the real National Palace was in Calles' guarded house outside of the city, because the ham-and-egg breakfasts continued at which Calles and Ambassador Morrow cordially entertained each other.

For the first time in the modern history of Mexican-American relations, the Ambassador was a man who had read that country's history and could talk the language of the other fellow's point of view. In turn, the Calles crowd were now men of property and could warm to Morrow's approach. He was a practical man of long views. He took the same attitude toward both the oil and Church deadlocks, sympathetically persuading the parties aggrieved by the Constitution to submit to its laws; in return, it was understood, their application would rest lightly. The foreign debt was scaled down and arrangements were made to meet interest payments on it and on the railroad obligations, in easier installments and with the prospect of course of a loan. "I make no pretense to passing any final judgments on Ambassador Morrow's actuations and policies in Mexico," wrote Dr. Eyler Simpson in his minutely scholarly study of Mexico's land problem; "I simply note the fact that coincident with his presence in Mexico the life went out of the revolution."

A new era was dawning, Mexico was told by the veterans of the Calles crowd. The revolution was achieved. Now must come stabilization, reconstruction. Capital was needed, would be welcomed and protected. Labor must listen to reason. Portes Gil, Morones' bitter, long-term enemy, pulled the patronage props out from under the CROM. This, in view of the discontent and insurgencies in its own ranks, dismembered the Federation. Labor would be better off, thought Portes Gil, if it spent less energy on strikes and concentrated on setting up co-operatives. He could point with pride to the Tampico dock workers' co-operative, which he had helped to start some years ago, as a solution to strike deadlocks. It was a prosperous transport and longshore company now. Unions led only to trouble; labor and capital should get together, if they only would, in co-operatives.

As for the agrarian program, since De Negri was again Minister of Agriculture, it moved. In 1929 more villagers got more land than in any previous year, but in December Calles came back from a trip to Europe and said in a New York interview that land distribution was a failure and that it should be stopped just as quickly as feasible. In due course peasants would get a chance to buy land, the haciendas would partition themselves, on easy payments.

This freed the Callistas from many political embarrassments but left them with only military and financial friends with which to make the elections. Pascual Ortiz Rubio, an engineer who had campaigned in the revolution and been a member of the Obregón cabinet, but a man with the personality of a ship's purser, was picked to be the front. A group of big generals rebelled, and were put down by Calles ruthlessly. Ortiz Rubio was inaugurated in February, 1930. Soon afterward he issued a stop order on land distribution. *Agraristas* dissatisfied with that perspective were disarmed and "pacified" by troops, sometimes forever and sometimes with a kind of implicit "Lie low, boys . . . wait a while."

Somebody threw a bomb at the President and bruised him. The prosperity program—salvation through capitalism—went ahead full blast. Industrialization sped and business flourished, and prices climbed, and climbed. The Callista construction company paved many streets and made a costly masterpiece, a tiled underpass for pedestrians. The favorite generals went halves in every kind of business, including plushy casinos. The most exclusive one in Mexico City was a big-stake place named "The Foreign Club."

The full effects of the world depression struck Mexico belatedly in 1932, choking exports. Jobs and wages dropped, there were no takers for peasant products, and there were some currency panics and runs for metallic coin on the national bank. Ortiz Rubio appointed Calles emergency man for the financial situation. Somebody fired at the President and wounded him in the jaw. Soon afterwards he resigned, and went to the United States to recuperate, remarking, "Believe it or not, gentlemen, being President is very difficult, very, very difficult." His place was taken, provisionally again, by General Abelardo Rodríguez, an energetic, experienced big businessman of the type we call enlightened. A study of wages and living standards was made, and the results embodied in a minimum wage law. In most cases the wages declared necessary by the panel of economists, physicians, and social scientists who made the survey were so far above what was being paid that little attempt was made to enforce the law. For the peasants, the list of essentials to life, beginning with eighteen hundred calories and four vitamins, and including a pair of blankets and perhaps one medical visit a year, added up, against what they had, to sheer fantasy. And though in Díaz days it had always been said that they didn't want much and would not know what to do with more than tortillas and beans (except get drunk), this did not seem to be true any more. Few of them had to travel far to see the landed and cattled benefits of revolution, for the chiefs.

No more mention was made of the stop law, and some credit was made available to peasants who had received their land. Funds were spread to public works in the smaller towns. New dams were started, and several highways were finished. Inter-village buses and trucks removed burdens from many Indian backs. The Pan-American Highway brought a balm of tourist dollars to a number of generals (including the President) who put up de luxe hotels, but a great many smaller and even smallest enterprisers also benefited. Americans and Mexicans, who had known each other, dubiously, only through the dealings of carpetbaggers and the resulting quarrels of the two governments, met by the thousand as individuals, and found each other childlike but nice. American tastes became the height of fashion: neon lights, cocktail bars, hotcakes, soft drinks, Virginia cigarettes. The President conversed in fluent English and pitched the first ball in baseball games. Wives of politicos bought mink coats and learned to play bridge; their mistresses bought Lincolns. And prices continued to climb.

The unions began to growl, federating toward the 1933 elections under the leadership of Vicente Lombardo Toledano, a University professor with a Savonarola face, who professed Marx and had once been a CROM lieutenant. Calles sheered to the wind and made speeches in which he said that foreign capital that couldn't get along with Mexican labor to labor's satisfaction could go back where it came from, and let the government and the workers run the plants for the national welfare. Land distribution was hurried. To continue in power, riding successfully through the elections, the Callistas had two choices: either old-fashioned terrorist military dictatorship financed from the United States, or a really popular candidate.

The Morrow-Calles hopes for money to finance the development of capitalism had so far borne only good will. So there was really only one alternative—to find a man with the following qualifications: He must be friendly enough to ensure continuity for the "ins," yet make the irritated eighty per cent believe that National Revolutionary Party meant something more than the way people read its initials—Plutarco Needs to Rob. He must be a man with a good revolutionary record, who had not got rich by it, must be acceptable to the army and liked by the peasants and labor and, above all, not identified with Callismo.

A platform had to be worked out too, but this was less difficult: just put everything in. So the revolution was revived in a program called the Six Year Plan (length of the new presidential term), which projected, on a wide and flowery landscape, the picture outlined in the Constitution. The Plan would advance socialization and co-operatives, and at the same time protect legitimate business and "constructive" capital, particularly Mexican enterprise; would help the farmers and distribute land. Its leitmotif was "something for everybody, and Mexico for the Mexicans." All the orators bore down on this message: "Let no one challenge the revolution. Its defender is the PNR and the PNR has a program and a candidate, a poor man's candidate, General Lázaro Cárdenas."

He was—as was later discovered—a dark horse even to those who pushed through his nomination in the inner councils of the PNR. His backers were the Obregonista and labor and agrarian wings of the party, with Portes Gil the background Farley. The Callistas nervously resisted and then got on the bandwagon too. To most Mexicans Cárdenas was just a name. He was liked by the soldiers, had learned as a guerrilla how to *madrugar*—to dawn (Mexican slang for move fast and strike first). In his home state, Michoacán, he had as governor advanced land reform and school building enough to be very popular, and he lived modestly. No one could say for sure what went on in his pear-shaped Indian head, for his custom was to listen, his full red mouth slightly open, his face deadpan, his hot topaz-colored eyes intent.

The campaign speeches, written by party torchbearers, sound wildly inflammatory if read in English, but in Mexico City they were so much cloth off the familiar bolt. What was different was that Cárdenas made the speeches in the small towns and villages. He campaigned as if in war, fast, in constant bivouac, getting his car over the roughest roads, going beyond that on horseback. In such places what he said sounded like Madero and Zapata come back to earth again, in the person of a man whom the peasants called simply Lázaro, ending in a cry of "Lázaro . . . father . . . help us!"

The first official act of President Cárdenas was to refuse to live in Chapultepec, the presidential mansion that was once Maximilian's castle. Next he closed the casinos, regardless of how high up in the PNR were the owners. The Foreign Club was dismantled, to be used as an orphanage or school. Next he ordered the National Telegraph to take, free, for one hour daily, any message anybody wished to send him. In the presidential waiting rooms and patio a strict rule of precedence was applied: the barefoot and ragged first. He kept on traveling, as if still campaigning, taking a couple of secretaries and two or three of the hardier cabinet members such as Mújica and Ramón Beteta. No one knew whether the trip would last a week or three months, nor from day to day where they would go next. When the President arrived in town—always a small town—he arrived unannounced. So instead of reviewing parades from a balcony, he and his ministers inched afoot through the crowd pressing forward to see him, touch him, tell him their troubles.

He would sit in the courthouse for about ten hours a day for several days, listening. Every evening the secretaries took a list: a pump here, a bridge there, such and such orphans of a revolutionary soldier to be sent to school in the capital, an agronomist to come from the city to fight this or that pest. He appeared to believe that the public funds should be put at once at the disposal of the public. "The revolution was in the gutter," said Cárdenas diffidently to this writer. "It is necessary to raise it up."

The current joke was that one morning while dispatching business in the capital his secretary laid a list of urgent matters, and a telegram, before him. The list said: *Bank reserves dangerously low.* "Tell the Treasurer," said Cárdenas. *Agricultural production failing.* "Tell the Minister of Agriculture." *Railways bankrupt.* "Tell the Minister of Communications." *Serious message from Washington.* "Tell Foreign Affairs." Then he opened the telegram, which read: "My corn dried, my burro died, my sow was stolen, my baby is sick. Signed, Pedro Juan, village of Huitzlipituzco."

"Order the presidential train at once," said Cárdenas. "I am leaving for Huitzlipituzco."

The ten per cent of acreage that had been figured the maximum that could be distributed was passed and nearly doubled. Wherever there was a large land-workers' strike or a chronically violent conflict, Cárdenas arrived, invoked the Constitutional principle of national welfare versus private property, and settled the dispute with full application of the agrarian law. The owners were left the house and nucleus of the plantation— the "small holding" size, around six hundred acres—and usually also whatever industrial plant there might be, such as sugar refineries. Some profited greatly by this, as it left them in an industrial position and relieved of the worst labor problem. Others resigned themselves to farming intensively what was left, shifting at the same time into commerce and manufacturing. A few even assisted at the act of distribution, housing the President as their guest. Many had sons in the government service, as engineers usually, and either because the struggle had gone on so long or because the younger generation had influenced the elders, the attitude among the majority of Mexican landholders was a shrugged "Well . . . it was inevitable . . . perhaps necessary . . . but he's going at it too fast."

The Minister of Agriculture, Tomás Garrido Canabal, was a man who owned plantations himself, some of which he ran as "co-operatives" in his home state, Tabasco; and who deployed red-shirted "legions" on landing fields cleared of jungle, parading them to festivals at which saints' images were smashed; and who always traveled in a private plane, with an American pilot, a tommygun, and a batch of pretty secretaries. But the head of the newly created independent Agrarian Department was a have-not, a very young fellow with the ruthless immobile face of an Aztec image, and his headquarters always looked as if a peasant congress were in session. Teams of agronomists, surveyors, and organizers streamed out from here and rushed around the country in station wagons, speeding up the distribution process. Money was poured into a new chain of government banks set up specifically to finance, advise, and oversee the co-operatives and collectives through which it was hoped that peasants owning a very few acres might be able to produce enough to eat and a surplus to sell in the needy market. Irrigation projects, rural roads, agricultural machinery drew on these banks; manufacturing and industrial co-operatives drew on yet another new bank; all this, and schools, and a busy rural sanitation corps, and a host of other enterprises kept the National Treasury overdrawn.

Some of the enterprises were gigantic. In the north, almost the whole Laguna cotton zone, which had been developed by irrigation and was owned chiefly by foreign capital, was turned into a vast co-operative community, made up of many smaller self-governing producers' and consumers' co-operatives. It was said that in the hands of ignorant peasants, Mexico's cotton production could be considered wrecked; and the jolt was indeed terrific. But after the first dislocations, the figures averaged somewhat better than before. They gave no clue, though, to the elementary changes that were taking place. Curious sociologists checked, when the first profits were distributed to one co-operative, what the money went for, expecting to find the same sort of splurge as at a mining camp—with liquor the number one item. Number one instead turned out to be house furnishings, with American mattresses at the head of the list. In the community hospital young Dr. José Godínez Rivera was carrying on a long, wily duel with a witch who was losing her ailing clientele. One day she came to the doctor herself, asking in a roundabout way for medical advice. Enough people saw her there to question her spells thereafter. Her supremacy was gone.

An agrarian engineer, new on the job at the bank, started out to make rounds in the villages, expecting simply to give orders to the directing committees, like a manager to foremen. He found himself instead explaining why another tractor had not yet been made available, and why work mules had been purchased at such a figure, and why he personally could not diagnose a certain plant blight, and so on through the perspiring hours. A train conductor who made the regular run from El Paso liked to talk about the "experiment" each time he came through. "No doubt about it," he would say, "Mexico is coming up. Over there in the United States, they have their troubles ahead of them yet; we've been through ours. Things are going down over there. Here, we're coming up."

Before-and-after pictures of most Mexican villages would not show any great change. But once upon a time a stranger who happened to ride in would find deserted streets, closed doors, rustlings in the houses; famished dogs like coyotes snarled at his horse's heels, and, if he dismounted, some elder with suspicion on his face, fear in his eyes, would inquire his business. Today no one, not even the women and children, hides. Doors stay open, people keep on working, small boys tag along asking to act as guides. The women, if they get a chance, like to show the community prides, which are likely to be: the public corn-grinder, run by an old car motor at the rate of a few pennies for the day's supply of dough; the pump; the school and perhaps even—high point of the itinerary—showers and toilets; and finally, maybe, the flourishing fields and the good adobe house, the squashes and beans and corn and tomatoes and peppers and roses and morning-glories of a family who have had their *ejido* for some years. Inside the house, in the place of honor, an article of great luxury may be pointed out—an American meat-grinder, being used, instead of the ancient stone metate, to make tortilla dough. "There," someone is likely to say very grandly, "that is the aspiration of every woman's heart."

The sharpest change was intangible. Fear left the have-nots and was distributed to the haves. The new policy—solve conflicts by expropriation —was not limited to land. It was applied boldly to industry too, affecting a number of small mines and plants, so presently there were few disputes the arbitration boards could not settle as soon as they began, to the advantage of the workers and regardless, virtually, of demands. Even the Ford plant went closed shop without a murmur. The CTM labor federation built out of the wreck of the CROM, plus, and headed by Toledano was now mightier than the CROM when Morones and Calles were Siamese twins. It was the nightmare of business because of what tomorrow might bring. Heads of big enterprises, particularly those that were foreign-owned, gritted their teeth and signed contracts that were far beyond what they thought reasonable; much less than American workers got in the United States, the Mexicans pointed out; but much more than Mexicans in Mexico had earned before. If no curb were put to this, they thought, anything could happen. Hadn't it been the intention of the revolutionaries, ever since Carranza days, to drive the gringos out? And Toledano might seem to talk sensibly, but who could doubt that if Stalin instructed, he would perform according to plan?

Toledano had no government position, but he ran a bigger, smoother-working monopoly than Morones, reaching much beyond profit. The top machinery of the CTM was Communist party controlled, in much the same undercover way as Communists worked with John Lewis in the CIO. There were inner pipelines from the boss clique to certain ministries and departments—Education, for instance, where patronage was party controlled. Government employees and teachers were themselves members of unions. Intellectuals who didn't hew to the party line were frozen out of jobs; inside the unions, unsubmissive members who bucked the top clique might be shoved out of the union, and without a card there was no job. Cárdenas, no fellow traveller (he granted asylum to Trotsky), nevertheless gave the CTM full backing. Organized labor would have to throw off its bosses from inside, he thought. But regardless of political racketeering, the unions must be independently strong. "Some of my best friends," he said, "tell me that if only I would use a strong hand on labor my difficulties would be over. They say we could get all the money we need for the country from the United States. But tell me, a government-in-business that puts a strong hand on the unions, what is that? Fascism."

Against this background the oil companies stupidly refused to make terms with the unions on renewal contracts. The union demands were lengthy and glittering, and the companies said they were not financially able to meet them. There was a difference, between what the companies said it would cost and what the government thought, of several million pesos. Cárdenas offered to set the sum aside in escrow, as guarantee that the cost would not go over what his experts said. The companies refused. At bottom the real issue was power, as it had been all along, and now there was this crucial detail: the unions demanded that all but top executives be subject to the closed shop, which meant that engineers, bookkeepers, and many other technicians (now Mexican because of an earlier law limiting the number of foreigners any company could employ) would be on the other side of the fight, with the deadly ammunition of inside information. As a matter of fact, many were already union members or allies, close to the leadership. Their trained intelligence gave the union drive a

cutting edge, and their bitterness supplied more steam; for Mexicans working in Mexico for foreign companies were still barred from many opportunities and privileges, and ranked as social inferiors in a thousand minor,
humiliating ways.

The dispute went through the boards to the courts, to a special labor
board where a battery of government statisticians buried the Díaz-days oil
lawyers in reports, charts, records, calculations, and hair-raising descrip-
tions and photographs of oil-company housing and sanitation. On the basis
of this material, which ran to thousands of pages and was not apparently
grasped by counsel for the companies, the board decided against them, and
the case went to the Supreme Court. This body decided against the companies too, of course. They refused to submit. The point was now, who
is boss?

It was the peak of a long struggle much like the Church-State feud for
power that had culminated when Juárez expropriated the Church. The law
gave the oil unions the right to enforce the decision through a strike. This
would tie up all production, would hamper the railroads seriously, and
affect all industry. What might come with a long, violent conflict was un-
foreseeable but very dangerous. Cárdenas "dawned." He declared the oil
situation was a national emergency, and in the name of common welfare
against private interest, he invoked the Constitution and expropriated.

Almost at once great sums were drained from the banks, and silver purchasing by the U.S. Treasury was suspended. But the Mexican economic
system is still so much on a cash-and-carry basis that it absorbed the shock,
as the spongy ground of the capital absorbs earthquakes. There was no
panic. The propaganda of the oil men aimed at two things: to convince
Americans that Mexico was in chaos, that confiscation of everything was
in the cards, that the oil industry was being wrecked by clumsy Mexican
labor, and that it was even impossible to travel, that tourists could get no
gas for their cars. In Mexico it aimed to teach the Mexican people that

Cárdenas economics had snarled all production, had destroyed agriculture, was bringing poverty to all. In both countries the oil-company publicists carefully avoided argument about the oil-company story itself. This was considered beside the point. The issues emphasized were the welfare of Mexican life and property, with strong emphasis on maladministration and graft in the land program.

This convinced many people that "Cárdenas is going too fast," but made no friends for the oil companies. Even the archbishop, sensing the quality of popular feeling, declared that it was the patriotic duty of all Mexicans to support their government. From this advantageous position agitation was started to change the Constitution's educational doctrine to bring it more in line with Catholic beliefs.

In Washington, despite anguish at jeopardized property rights not only in Mexico but throughout Latin America, it had been realized that: (1) the club was futile; (2) a peaceful and friendly Mexico was a vital necessity to the people of the United States; (3) the everyday Mexican phrase *por las buenas, sí* (in a nice way, yes) is the way business is done. So there was no *go* light to the opposition.

Cedillo, a revolutionary chief who had become a feudal lord in San Luis Potosí, with his private chapel, private army, and even a little air force, proclaimed a crusade to defend religion, land, and the sacred rights of property from the atheistic bolshevistic government. Here too Cárdenas "dawned." The peasants on the Cedillo land were told that it was really theirs, and the chief was astonished that no revolutionary army materialized. Hence no more backing either. He was caught in a few weeks, up in the hills with less than a dozen men. When Calles, of whose machine Cárdenas had made debris, muttered for print something like what Cedillo had said, he was bundled out of bed one night—supposedly in the middle of reading *Mein Kampf*—and flown to California. General Juan Andreu Almazán, rocking placidly on the porch of his military headquarters in

Monterrey and making plans to be the next president, drawled: "Fighting
. . . that's all over. People have land, there is work, there is money . . .
Who would follow?" Then, thoughtfully, "But if the United States goes
to war, we're in the soup."

The smartest oil company, Sinclair, settled its claim for eight million
dollars, the valuation of its investments and plants, relinquishing its claim
to the subsoil. The others held out for property value plus subsoil value,
and the government held out the Constitution.

General Manuel Ávila Camacho was picked in
1940 as the candidate of the revamped official party for almost the opposite set of qualities, under opposite circumstances, as had sent Cárdenas to
the top. Capital wanted its fears put down. Cárdenas had gone far enough
so that beyond, even the holdings of *políticos* and generals might be im-
periled. Ávila Camacho, Minister of War in the Cárdenas cabinet, was a
name less real than the two other military who wanted the chair too:
General Gildardo Magaña, who had been a Zapatista and was a close
friend of Cárdenas; and General Juan Andreu Almazán, who had also
been a prominent guerrilla chief and had in the Calles period become a big
businessman and real estate operator. Ávila Camacho had, of course, a
record of service in the revolution, he had been an administrator under
Cárdenas. He came from the same home town as Toledano and was on
fairly friendly terms with him. Personally he was known as a good Catholic, a man tender to the susceptibilities of big business, since his brother
Maximino, one of the important capitalist generals and governor of
Puebla, was the good friend of the pious Spanish money that dominates
that state.

None of these were good talking points for the majority of the Mexican
public, while the propertied minority was much more devoted to Almazán.
But Almazán would have his own boys to feed, and would probably bring

back to power many Callistas, possibly Calles himself. The continuity that every administration seeks could be provided by Ávila Camacho, steering with caution to the middle of the road. To Cárdenas he seemed a better guarantee than Almazán perhaps, than even yielding to the outward and inward demands of money; the clock he had so rapidly spun forward would not be set too far back. Besides, north of the border Almazán was looked upon with a shade of doubt. When war came he might practice the same sort of unfriendly neutrality followed in World War I by Carranza. Furthermore, he had been a student in Germany and was thought to have some admiration for Nazi methods, while the fascism of the Franco men close to Maximino was not considered a disadvantage. The Nazis detailed agents, blondes, and money to campaign in both camps.

The struggle was sharp and bloody. Almazán promised stabilization, guarantees to capital, amendment of the Constitution to cancel socialist education, peace, and no surrender to the oil companies. He was supported by the wealthy and the middle class, and all political Catholics; and by many of the military, apprehensive of Toledano's recently organized labor militia, and of Cárdenas' peasant millions armed as Agrarian Reserves. And he got an enormous protest following, including even extreme leftists. This turnout, which drew on the unions and peasants too, was not enthusiasm for Almazán nor rancor against Cárdenas personally, but opposition to his crowd, on these counts: (1) racketeering all down the line in government projects; (2) business fear; (3) racketeering plus demagogy in the unions and peasant leagues; (4) abuse of power by the Communist party whips who ran most of the unions; (5) the spoils–patronage–party-line combine.

For his part, Ávila Camacho started without an aggressive program, simply as an affable Cárdenas man with army blessing, offering ease to all, forecasting a sort of NEP period. In the midst of the campaign he attended Mass showily, and made this the central plank of his platform: "I am a believer." The Catholic vote was already Almazán's, and clerical support heretofore had been no help in revolutionary politics. But the act of faith had great export value. It reassured the U.S. State Department, where the Good Neighbor policy (for reasons geared to investment and to the workings of the Democratic party machine) has been operating along the same lines as relations with Vichy, Franco, Salazar of Portugal, and other such autocrats in countries where the Church has a big stake; the policy being that such rulers are preferable to liberals and democrats. In Mexico, Ávila Camacho's declaration was good news to all Catholics, of course: the end of civil-religious struggle, the reunion of Church and State. It was a windfall for Franco's Falange and the cluster of powerful leagues using religion to build fascism from within, and to fight the revolution, and to fight friendship with the United States. Whoever was president, they would have the inside track. The Nazis happily dismantled their own apparatus and climbed into the knightly armor of the Franco-Falange-Jesuit "reconquest crusade."

Clearly at issue, besides the direction the revolution would take, was Mexico's place when war reached America. The two interlocked, for the Axis hand in America meant that the revolution too would be blotted out. The international struggle, going on elsewhere already in open war, merged with the Mexican struggle—was the same thing in world-wide form. Totalitarians hurried to lay in the political armament that would direct or paralyze military action and production, and the heaviest artillery was this: "You have nothing to fear from anyone but the United States, which is a Protestant, irreligious country seeking to destroy Mexican tradition, and to assimilate Mexico for the benefit of Wall Street."

Many lives were lost in the violence that preceded and accompanied the elections. If all those who wanted to vote had been able to get their ballots recorded, possibly Almazán would have won. At the end of the day Cárdenas, having made rounds of the shambles at the polls, said wearily,

"Mexico is not yet a democracy." Almazán departed for the United States and refrained from the customary revolt. Vice-President Wallace, innocent of the furor caused by such a visit on such an occasion, attended the inauguration.

Soon after that event, President Ávila Camacho spoke classic phrases: The revolution is finished. Its aims have been achieved. The era of reconstruction and stabilization is here. Land distribution need not continue; the agrarian reform is accomplished. Henceforth progress will come by evolution. Capital is welcome and can be sure of guarantees. There was a revival of fashionable devotion, and for the first time since before Juárez, government officials made public point of piety. The glittering names of two generations back, refugeed from France, Italy, and Spain, repossessed the capital. Shady bluebloods and tycoons who knew the details of why France (and other places) fell, established their headquarters in Mexico City, followed by fashionable dressmakers, purveyors of gems and furs, and dealers in concessions, contracts, and international plots. The Spanish colony, mostly Franco supporters, banqueted the President. The Sinarquistas, a peasant league based on ex-Cristeros, which says it defends religion, property, and the fatherland against bolshevism (thus wrapping the Nazi-Franco formula in the Mexican flag), petitioned the President for permission to colonize on strategic Magdalena Bay, and got a favorable reply and moved right in. The leftist Minister of Education was removed, a middle-roader came in, and he was then supplanted by an army officer who thought that technique and science should be discarded in favor of the classics. Said he: "There can be no education in Mexico without the sign of the Cross behind it."

Toledano's CTM, without government support now, fell apart from inner pressures and, as expected, conservative leaders began to tinker a new federation nearer official favor. Police machine-gunned petitioners from the munitions-plant employees in front of the President's house. Negotiations through the U.S. State Department to settle the oil and other disputes pending began to proceed smoothly now toward a loan, a substantial amount for irrigation, industrialization, and other government needs. A treaty was signed and the money, big money, began to arrive. A mixed committee of experts examined the oil figures and awarded an offer to the companies, of about ten per cent of their claims, which was neither accepted nor refused. The manager of the American Smelting and Refining Co. was made cultural contact man for Washington's good will program. Five new banks opened, and the heart of the city was leased by a suddenly frenzied bourse. The inrush of capital, plus war production, unleashed a boom that made the oil days look like chickenfeed. Prices, rising for some time, leaped now. Food staples, never plentiful, grew meager. And the word was spread, and believed widely, that the government was sold to Washington, had turned its back on its own people, and was herding the nation to war.

Severiano Pérez, who works in the gasoline station in the town of San Andrés, was enjoying the evening on a plaza bench when he heard that Mexico was at war. With his three cronies, the municipal clerk, the blacksmith, and a dealer in hides and tallows, he had been discussing Chinese strategy in the light of their boyhood experiences in the revolutionary army. The war news blared confusedly from the radio in the Spaniard's general store up the street. Only disconnected phrases could be heard on the plaza: "Citizen President Manuel Ávila Camacho . . . In this grave hour . . ." and the name of the tanker that had been torpedoed, the newspapers said by the Germans but, many sceptics asserted, really by the Americans.

Men rose, moving unhurriedly to the store, bunching at the entrance. Murmured commentaries took on the hoarseness of emotion as it grew real that Mexico, unbelievably Mexico, *fatalmente* was plunged in the world war. Severiano and the others in the crowd outside caught that fact

only from the tumbled words of the radio announcer. He responded automatically. He raised his head and yelled, "*¡Viva Mexico!* Death to the
gringos! *¡Viva la revolución!*" and the crowd chorused full blast "*¡Viva-
a-a-a-a-a! ¡Muera-a-a-a-a!*" The yells fell apart in bewildered mutters,
however, when the telegrapher, a union man, pushed through from inside
the store, shouting "Idiots! Imbeciles! We're against Germany! . . . Mexico
is on the side of the Allies! Don't you understand, the gringos are on our
side . . . We're fighting fascism! *¡Viva la revolución . . . !*" On the other
side of the crowd where the women were, an old, cracked voice cried "God
preserve us! God free us and keep us in his holy hand . . . !" and then in a
strange, startled tone, "Who would have ever told me that I would come
to be praying for gringos . . . !"

That, for the first time in the history of the two republics, their guns
would be aimed in the same direction was accepted thus dubiously in the
small places. In the capital and the larger cities, the dominant reaction
among the well-off was rage, and a favorite commentary on the torpedoed
tanker was that it had no business carrying oil for the gringos anyway.
Only a portion of the professionals and intellectuals, leftists, Cárdenas
men, and a very few of the military, were sincerely able to put their fear of
the United States second to the menace of the Axis. Labor followed their
line of reasoning. The Communists put away the set of "Down with
American imperialism!" banners they had used until attack on Russia
ended the Stalin-Nazi pact, and unfurled the other set which read, "Down
with fascism! Defend the fatherland! Defend the Soviet Union!"

At the same time as he declared war the President took over extraordi-
nary powers and suspended the Constitution's provisions for civil liberties.
Soon afterward he again spoke classic phrases, the nervous formula this
time. The revolution, he said, marched on forever. Agrarian reform would
continue. He explained to foreign reporters that he was a socialist, and
that Mexico was a socialist state. General Cárdenas—the Brutus in the

picture, whatever his own thoughts—was made Chief of Defense. An astounding Exhibit A was presented to the nation: a line-up, on the balcony of the National Palace, of the President and his living predecessors, Calles and Cárdenas and Rodríguez and Ortiz Rubio and Portes Gil, and forgotten De la Huerta. On the eve of trouble, generals and *políticos* always send messages of support to the central government. Mexicans recognize it as a virtual announcement of uprising. This was a dramatized version, and a warning: Premature. No green light. Even so, when the draft was announced, some time later, little gangs of resisters preached and rioted in some small places; and somebody tried to blow up the President's train.

Since most of these belligerents were known to be affiliated with the Sinarquista and other Catholic semi-fascist groups, Archbishop Luis Martínez, whose friendliness to the government was not shared by the majority of the clergy or the devout upper class, found it necessary to declare that it was the duty of all good Catholics to support their government. It was the first time such a thing had been said, thus flatly, since the days when Mexico was ruled by the Spanish crown.

Meanwhile other crises kept coming to a head. The long-limping railroads, for instance, being overhauled with American money and under the direction of a commission of American experts, brought on a clash between the government and the experts on the one hand and the railroad union on the other, with the President threatening to militarize the lines and then holding off when the union offered to work out its own reorganization plan. Much point was made of the frequent wrecks and disasters, which had been going on for many years, due primarily to the physical condition of the lines; publicity blamed them on recalcitrant labor. Tensions due to this and similar conflicts churned up increasing uneasiness, and again and again officials were asked to promise clearly that Mexicans would not be shipped to fight in foreign lands.

Inside the "government of national unity" there is a struggle between Cárdenistas and fascists who love money from any source, no objection to dollars either. Between the two there are many agile opportunists who swing wherever the current of power seems to be heading. The Cárdenas men, mostly brain-trusters of socialist beliefs, and the people they influence, are our only steady allies. In their hands the foreign affairs department has, with some trepidation, cut Mexico away from its traditional system of seesawing a hostile European power against the United States. They hope to replace that sort of protection by building a federation of American republics in which each one would be as safe from the outside, and from each other, as the states in a republic. Or, failing that, to set up a Latin American bloc to counterpoise the power of the United States.

Because of Mexico's immediate revolutionary past, it is something like a school for liberal policy-makers in many other Latin American republics; its moral leadership is far beyond its size. Therefore it has had an enormous effect on the conduct of the war, for without its diplomatic work, the line-up of twenty-one American republics against the Axis could not have been achieved.

The Mexican people, the majority unreached by press and radio, are not convinced that they have any real stake in this war. They sympathize with us because we are in danger, and our strength is awakening great admiration. But they fear their alliance with us. Not invasion from us any more— they believe Roosevelt really means his Good Neighbor pledge. But they fear being cheated, through our domination, of what was achieved by the million lives given up in the revolution. Our record, after all, has been, there and in other Latin American countries, to strengthen those who gain by strangling the Four Freedoms. Our government shows greater and greater friendliness, and gives concrete help, as administrations swing farther and farther right, and this time, with each step the administration has taken dangerously far right, we have progressively reached the warmest relations since Díaz. The Mexican people therefore identify counter-revolution with American influence.

Independence, complete isolation of any country's affairs from all others, is now recognizably everywhere a fiction. On the American continent the power of the United States affects how many peoples live, and how they are ruled. Mexico, bucking that, holds the center of the Latin American stage. Thus the same question that has defeated England on so many fronts—the question of India—the terrible question of have-nots—"What is your democracy to us?"—confronts us next door, and through Mexico south in the rest of the continent. A dangerous question if answered, not by the good sense and straight decency of the American people, but by tricky business and political deals.

The answer we shape will determine whether the wind that swept Mexico returns as a tornado—a grimly furious, desperate tornado, endangering much more than investments. Our answer decides also to what extent the other peoples of Latin America are actively our allies or passively our enemies. And already the same sort of question is facing us, with sharp military urgency, elsewhere in the world.

The United States is a nation that most of the world thinks it can trust. In Latin America our position is equivocal; it is just being discovered that the American people are not buzzards. Our standing, influence toward the kind of world we want to live in, and even our safety, depend on how many of us clearly grasp the question put in the Mexican story, and how honestly we apply its meaning. It is not alien to us. In the history of the American Revolution there was a flag, much like the Mexican flag, with a serpent on it, and four living words that tell the record of both peoples: Don't Tread on Me.

The Photographic
History of the
Mexican Revolution

1. In the year 1910 there was a Strong Man of the Americas advertised in all the world, and his name was Porfirio Díaz of Mexico . . .

2. The aged man had been sitting for thirty-four years—with one brief interim—in the presidential chair. Round him, like cherubim and seraphim in a religious picture, there was a group of courtly, elderly men who had long since done away with politics and devoted themselves to nourishing business. This, they said, was the true science of government; problems of state were handled scientifically; they were called the *científicos* . . .

(Standing, at the right of Díaz, is Limantour. Ramón Corral is sitting at the right hand of Díaz.)

3. At his right hand—pale, scrupulous, and faultless as a tailor's dream—hovered
Don José Ives Limantour, primate of the holy of holies, Secretary of Finance.

4. Near him also was the Vice-President, Don Ramón Corral, who could have won the vote by acclamation as the most hated man in Mexico. Corral was known as the money maker in the slave trade in the tropics, as king of another slave trade in the capital, and himself its victim, with his disease so far advanced he had at most two years to live.

5. Near him also was Archbishop Mora y del Río, primate of the Mexican hierarchy, presiding over a Church fabulously rich since the days of the conquest.

6. Each time Díaz reassumed his dictatorial position—re-election followed re-election with monotonous calm—the Kaiser, the Mikado, and all important potentates flashed messages of joy. The Kaiser's portrait, executed in imperially strongman style, hung on the wall . . .

7. . . . in the audience chamber in the National Palace in Mexico City . . . which also contained a cuspidor in one corner for the convenience of visitors and promoters.

8. Order reigned. The peasants abased themselves before men on horseback, murmuring "Go with God." The roads were patrolled by *rurales*, well-mounted active men in dove-gray uniforms, tightly buttoned with silver. Plantation owners and the prosperous people in small communities loved them . . . villagers and hacienda workers had other emotions, since it was the *rurales* who hustled recruits for the army, or tied suitable prospects into the gangs shipped to the tropics—where labor was short-lived and plantation owners were willing to pay for able-bodied men at twenty-five pesos a head. It was the *rurales* who dispensed justice among the cacti according to the precepts laid down in Díaz' famous telegram: "Catch in the act, kill on the spot."

9. Peace reigned . . . in the northern deserts of Sonora . . .

10. Peace reigned in the towns . . .

11. Peace reigned in the buzzard-infested streets of Veracruz . . .

12. Peace reigned on the cattle ranges . . .

13. Peace reigned on the great haciendas, where the peasants ploughed with oxen
. . . using wooden plows . . .

14. Peace reigned in the missions . . .

15. Everywhere peace reigned and . . . for 90% of the population . . . the blessings of poverty also. It was Mexico's misfortune, said Limantour and the *científicos*, to try to progress with such a burden upon it: more than three-fourths of the population nearly pure Indian . . .

16. . . . irresponsible . . .

17. . . . lazy. Such beings could never perform, surely could not claim, participation in the acts of government. Let them work and keep the peace.

18. It was a safe land in which to do business. Cases involving a foreigner against a Mexican were decided according to the principle that the foreigner must be right, unless word came from Don Porfirio, exceptionally, to discover otherwise. Every American living and working in Mexico, from plant manager to gang foreman and oil driller, and every company that had American money in it—even if it were only one red cent, said the American Embassy (an imposing mansard structure with the American eagle blazoned over the gateway)—had the right to this same kind of extra-territorial immunity.

19. In the remotest places judges understood the fine points of these usages, and could interpret skilfully the precept taught by the United States State Department —presided over by the great Philander Knox of Pittsburgh—that Americans were guests and must be spared the judicial annoyances unavoidable to Mexicans.

20. The American Ambassador, Henry Lane Wilson, a corporation lawyer, was the resident agent of the great and distant power.

21. "Revolutions," said one of the *científicos*, "occur according to natural social law. And that law is that governments break down when they cannot pay their bills." Of this condition there was no sign. The Treasury had a surplus of 62,483,119 pesos, gold.

22. The railroads, to which Benito Juárez had objected in the 1870's, fearing easy invasion from the United States, had at last been built, tunneling the great mountain ranges . . .

23. . . . and spanning rocky gorges, and had been merged through a Limantour maneuver into a national company, stock-controlled by the government, run by American management.

24. It was a land where men of imagination and money could be as Midas. There was the Englishman, Weetman Pearson, who had connected the Atlantic with the Pacific with the Tehuantepec Railway—which he also operated—and had dredged the harbor of Veracruz and built the port works. Mr. Pearson, afterward Sir Weetman Pearson, had found oil and signed a concession with the government over the vastest rich deposits—and had now become Lord Cowdray.

(Lord Cowdray, in the straw hat, walking with Lord Aberdeen.)

25. There was William Randolph Hearst, who owned hundreds of thousands of acres of Mexican land . . .

26. There were the Guggenheims . . . who had mines in many places, smelters at Monterrey . . . San Luis Potosí . . .

(This picture of Meyer Guggenheim and his seven sons was taken not long after "Exemption from all municipal and state taxes [was] granted Sr. Daniel Guggenheim and the company or companies he may organize, on the capital he may invest in this city"—the city of Monterrey.) Left to right: Benjamin, Murry, Isaac, Meyer, Dan, Sol, Simon and William.

27. There were other capitalists who owned the Ojuela mine in Durango. Other foreigners owned other mines, smelters, and metals . . . gold, silver, lead, copper . . . in Guanajuato, the Silver City of the World, in Pachuca, in a score of towns . . .

28. At intervals the Strong Man journeyed about the country to inspect the mines, the smelters, the plantations which foreign capital and the concessionaires had brought to such a golden prosperity under the benediction of Finance Minister Limantour. The Strong Man, the son of an innkeeper of Oaxaca, of Indian descent . . .

29. . . . had married, late in life, Doña Carmelita, the pious daughter of Romero Rubio, a Spaniard and one of the great concessionaires, a power in railroads, in metropolitan real estate, owner of a great hacienda.

30. From the palace of Chapultepec . . .

31. . . . overlooking Mexico City . . .

32. . . . the Strong Man and Mme. Díaz presided over a brilliant and gaudy society whose mansions fronted a tree-lined boulevard, the Paseo de la Reforma . . .

33. . . . who entertained at the Spanish Casino . . .

34. . . . who, after Mass . . .

35. . . . rode in Chapultepec Park on Sunday mornings . . .

36. . . . and cheered when the aged Strong Man rode through the streets . . . On the whole, it was a cozy little *status quo*.

37. The great landed families spent a part of their time on their haciendas, estates worked by gangs of peons.

38. Existence there was sometimes euphemistically termed patriarchal. In the north, for example, the hacienda of the Terrazas family covered more than a million acres.

39. In the south the great planters lived in castellated abbeys . . . part church, part mansion, part fortress . . .

40. In the passage of time the ancient communal lands of the villages were swallowed up, the peasants harnessed to the factories—herded to work, sometimes, by a rider with a carbine.

There had been rebellions, strikes, attacks in newspapers. Troops put down the strikers, the *rurales* smothered the little rebellions, indiscreet newspapermen had time in the dungeon to think it over.

It seemed as though the regime, in its golden splendor of prosperity, was impregnable. Even though the anger and the hatred of centuries smoldered in the minds of the Indians, even though Mexicans sweated to belong to a middle class that scarcely existed, the government's bonds were at a premium on every exchange in the world. Few of the bondholders ever noticed that year by year the wealth was being concentrated in fewer hands. The bulk of the wealth was in the hands of less than one per cent of the people and most of that belonged to foreign investors . . . absentees . . .

41. All this had been described with cold meticulous rage in a book called *Los
grandes problemas nacionales*, published in 1909, written by a scholar named
Andrés Molina Enríquez. It became to the Mexican revolution what Rousseau's
Contrat Social was to the French, and more. It became the gospel of thousands upon
thousands of people who never heard of it, could not have read its simplest words.

42. There had been a number of strikes, planned ones like the strike the year before, in 1908, at the Río Blanco textile works, a business owned by Spanish and German capital. This strike was engineered—at a distance—by two mysterious brothers whose names were uttered in whispers. They were named Flores Magón—Ricardo and Enrique Flores Magón—exiles in St. Louis. Living from hand to mouth, they published a smudged and ill-printed weekly paper that was smuggled over the border into Mexico. They corresponded by stealth, sent messages by railway brakemen, and spent their time tapping the walls of the apparently impregnable dictatorship, looking for the weak places. Then came the Río Blanco strike. Don Porfirio sent the troops and it was put down with much blood. This was not like the other strikes . . . there was talk . . . Furthermore, there were signs . . . and omens . . .

43. In 1909 there was a violent eruption of Mt. Colima and the smoke and the ashes obscured the sky for many days. The Lord had promised to send Someone to do His work, the peasants said, and the powerful Old Ones would come out then and sweep the wicked away. These were the signs.

44. People in Mexico City—the knowing ones in the Banco de Londres y México and of course the *científicos*—understood about volcanic disturbances. They were explained in the books. But they did not hear about signs and omens. Next year, in 1910, came still another sign. People who could read learned that it was Halley's Comet and that there was nothing to fear. The scientists understood it.

(A street crowd in Mexico City watching the comet. The man with mustache and derby is Alfonso Cravioto, now in the Mexican diplomatic service. In the days of the comet he was an anti-Díaz agitator.)

45. But in the villages, where the glare destroyed the peace of the night and made the cattle uneasy, it was an announcement. The young were told by the old that it meant war, death, famine, and plague. The world of Don Porfirio and Doña Carmelita was coming to an end. It was best to confess and commune, for the Day of Judgment was at hand.

46. There were still other signs. In the northern part of Mexico lived a family named Madero. This family with its connections numbered one hundred and seventy-two male members who owned a million and a half acres in cotton, lumber, rubber, cattle; besides mines and smelters competing with the Guggenheims; besides wine and brandy distilleries, mortgages and real estate and provincial banks. One of the members of this clan was a bearded gentleman of the old Mexican school named Don Francisco Madero. Among his younger sons was . .

47. Francisco I. Madero. He was a small, quick-moving lawyer with kind eyes; he had his portion of the Madero estates, which he seemed to be dissipating in benevolent experiments . . . co-operatives, for example. He was a vegetarian, an ascetic; his heart was wrung by the condition of the Mexican people. He was a spiritualist, and the Ouija board had told him: "Francisco, one day you will be President of Mexico." He had just published a sensational book—*La sucesión presidencial* (The Presidential Succession). It dealt with effective suffrage, no re-election—mostly things that had been said long ago by Díaz himself, in the days when the example of Benito Juárez was still strong among men. But now the news of this man Madero was spread abroad. Village people understood that he lived in the capital or some such distant place and was married to a probably divine creature called the Constitution. Clearly he was not the same as other city people, whom it was always best to avoid mentioning.

48. If the Strong Man, eighty years old, heard of the signs and the omens, if he was annoyed by the effrontery of the young Madero in publishing his preposterous book, he gave no sign. He rode daily, sometimes accompanied by his son, and contemplated the approaching Centennial of Mexican Independence, which was to be celebrated with great splendor in September, 1910.

49. Great preparations for the celebration were made and the entire month of September was set aside as a holiday. There were new and resplendent uniforms for the bodyguards . . .

50. . . . the Palace was swept and garnished for the envoys who came—their expenses paid by the Mexican government—from every nation in the world. There were handsome presents from foreign monarchs. The visitors were shown the new public buildings . . .

51. . . . the Renaissance postoffice . . .

52. . . . the Italian marble opera house, begun to commemorate this anniversary . . .

53. . . . with its fabulous glass curtain already in place, a curtain made by Tiffany at the cost of—but why count the cost?

54. On the great day of all days, September 16, 1910 . . . floats rolled through the streets . . .

55. . . . a pageant depicting the history of Mexico since Moctezuma. And on the reviewing stand, presiding over the pageant, sat . . .

56. . . . the aged Strong Man with Doña Carmelita beside him. Very soon now, within a month, in October, 1910, his eighth presidential term would begin. Because of the Centennial celebration he had permitted young Madero to campaign against him in the elections. It had been disturbing . . . feverish excitement in the villages and cities, much speechmaking, turbulence, and so the Strong Man took precautions. Madero was jailed. He managed to escape, disguised as a brakeman, to the United States. This was unfortunate, but to insure Centennial quiet an embargo was laid on the Madero properties. The clan was frantic; they appealed to Limantour—who had gone to Paris to consolidate the Mexican debt—to save them. But some of the Maderos, particularly elder brother Gustavo, took a sporting chance to stave off family ruin. He threw himself into organizing Francisco's . . . revolution.

57. At the very moment that Don Porfirio was watching the Centennial processions, little groups of men were gathering in out-of-the-way places all over Mexico. They stole away from the villages and the ranches, assembling in secluded spots . . .

58. The gathering of the little bands was the rising of the wind, the beginning of the great storm that was about to sweep over Mexico. The Díaz regime, the closed circle of favorites, the *científicos*, had crushed the hopes of so many for so long that, as the regime began to totter, thousands, rich and poor, sniffed the wind and looked about them. Who would lead? Which way to success? Some wanted a full meal, some a new pair of pants; some wanted only a gun to blow to pieces a hated master. The ominous rumbling increased. There were a series of small risings in the towns, mercilessly suppressed.

59. More bands were gathering now . . . bigger bands . . . They said they were for Madero . . .

60. While the rebels were busy in the north, others were gathering in the south . . . Zapata's boys . . .

(Zapata is in the front row, sixth from the left, and wears a white hat and black coat. One of the posters on the wall advertises the Mexican Centennial celebration, which had occurred a few weeks before.)

61. In the capital, old Díaz feverishly worked to save the regime. The Strong Man went to the Palace offices every day, he telegraphed the provincial governors, he threatened, bribed, and cajoled. But every day brought worse news . . .

62. . . . trains stopped, passengers robbed and turned out to walk the ties.

63. On the 14th of March, 1911, Finance Minister Limantour arrived in New York from Paris and went at once to the Plaza Hotel. He knew almost to a cent how much money Madero had to finance his campaign and he knew that old man Madero was scared.

64. Downtown at the Imperial Hotel, at Broadway and 31st Street, was Dr. Vázquez Gómez. He was very short of money and was put to it for expenses. His particular errand was to prevent the panicstricken Madero family from losing their nerve and giving in to Limantour.

65. And across town at the Astor Hotel on Times Square was old man Madero and three of his sons—Gustavo, Gabriel, and Evaristo. Gustavo (on left) was the one who was talking for Francisco, who was waiting on the border to learn how the conferences turned out.

They made a sort of deal and Limantour set out for Mexico City to report to the old Strong Man and see if he couldn't manage to take over and patch up the regime and make concessions to the Maderos and other respectable malcontents at the same time. As for the riffraff, some way would be found to squash them.

66. Too late! By now the bands were gathering openly in the towns all over northern and middle Mexico . . .

67. Suddenly, after all the wavering, the maneuvering, and the waiting . . . shooting began. On the 10th of May, 1911, Americans climbed on the top of freight cars outside of El Paso to look across the Rio Grande and watch . . .

68. . . . the rebel snipers attack the city of Juárez and capture it from the Díaz garrison. Madero, across the border at last, watched the capture . . . made against his orders.

69. There were leaders other than Madero, but three of them overshadowed all the rest.

The first was the white-bearded Venustiano Carranza, governor of the State of Coahuila in northeastern Mexico. Sr. Carranza was a lawyer and a rancher. He had been a Senator in the Díaz Congress. He was for the middle man. He wanted the Church curbed, he wanted American capital to be told where to get off, he wanted to bust in on monopoly and let the Mexican businessmen, the industrialists, the professionals, and the farmers have a chance . . . under his direction. (Carranza on the left.)

70. The second was a man who had driven mule trains in Chihuahua and had been a cattle rustler. His name was Doroteo Arango, but for various reasons—one of them was that his name was on the books as a man the *rurales* wanted—he called himself Francisco Villa . . . after a famous old-time bandit . . . He was also called by the nickname Pancho . . . The men who followed him were cowpunchers, pack drivers from the north. (Villa on extreme right.)

71. The third was Emiliano Zapata, who came from the south, the old and rich and tropical state of Morelos. Zapata had once been kidnapped into the Díaz army. He was of dominant Indian blood and represented pure hatred for the great landed proprietors who for three hundred years had enslaved the Indians and, during the Díaz days, had taken away the last of the communal land which the Indians had held since the days of the Aztecs . . . The guerrilla bands, the little armies, of these men and the smaller chieftains, had finally swept away the last vestiges of Díaz's power.

72. Flushed with triumph, Madero entered Mexico City on the 7th of June, 1911. Two weeks before, in the dead of night, the aged Díaz and Doña Carmelita had boarded a train and made their way to Veracruz, where a boat was waiting. Limantour, Corral, and the rest of the charmed and gilded inner circle fled.

73. The mild idealist in Mexico City found himself pulled and hauled by the concessionaires, the foreign investors, the Díaz holdovers, who wanted their position
kept secure. Meanwhile . . .

(Photo taken in the audience chamber in the palace in Mexico City. Pino Suárez,
the new Vice-President, stands directly at Madero's right. The picture was taken in
the same spot where Díaz and his cabinet—second picture in the volume—were
photographed.)

74. Then, suddenly, there was trouble again. Some of the boys, restlessly watching the progress of affairs in the capital, were once more on the move.

75. One of Madero's generals was Pascual Orozco (extreme right, front row). After Díaz fled and the spoil was being divided—jobs, money, power—Orozco felt that he got the short end. He rebelled against Madero . . .

The group shows the northern revolutionary leaders before Madero's victory. The crowd was never together again. The chief figures in the front row, reading from the left, are Carranza, Vázquez Gómez (the man who stayed at the Imperial Hotel in New York), Madero, and Orozco. Standing in the back row, reading from the left, are Villa, Gustavo Madero and Francisco Madero Sr., his father (these two were the ones staying at the Astor Hotel during the negotiations with Limantour), and Colonel Garibaldi, the son of the Italian liberator, who is standing in the doorway.

76. The northerners were again sweeping the Federal troops before them . . . advancing on the capital . . . In the south the Zapata peasants were demanding results . . . lands returned now . . . The landholders were clamoring for a strong hand . . . and quietly conspiring . . . Concessionaires too were calling for iron measures . . . and doing business keeping the rebels armed . . . The military felt left out and were sullenly plotting a coup . . . Ambassador Henry Lane Wilson was scolding and threatening . . . and American troops were deployed on the Rio Grande . . . This was the sign the silk-hat and epaulette conspirators were waiting for . . .

(The generals who engineered the counter-revolution in February, 1913. Left to right, Mondragón, Huerta, Félix Díaz, and Blanquet.)

77. In desperation, Madero appointed as his commanding general a tough and ambitious old Indian killer, Victoriano Huerta, who had served many years in the Díaz army. He was given the job of crushing Orozco's rebellion . . . and did it. A new strong man had appeared. Gentlefolk sighed with relief.

(Huerta is sitting on the well curb. The young man in the gray suit and Stetson is Juan Andreu Almazán, a medical student who became a Maderista guerrilla.

Twenty-seven years later, in 1940, Almazán ran for President of Mexico.)

78. Madero refused to believe the generals could plot successfully against him. When they struck, Mexico City was their battleground . . . There followed the Tragic Ten Days of fighting in the streets between the loyal soldiers and the regiments of the conspirators. No one went abroad except under cover of a white flag.

79. Ambassador Wilson rode about the city, with a flag tied to the embassy automobile . . . negotiating . . . demanding and making arrangements . . . On the night of February 19, Blanquet, supposedly loyal, seized Madero in the Palace, without interference from Huerta, who was Madero's chief of defense . . .

80. Ambassador Wilson called the foreign diplomats together at the Embassy, introduced them to Huerta and other plotters, and told them of the new arrangements. Huerta would be (toast to Law and Order) provisional president.

(Wilson in the center with the gray mustache. Huerta at his right.)

81. "And what," said Manuel Márquez Sterling, the Cuban Ambassador, "are you going to do with Madero?" Ambassador Wilson shrugged. Intercession was made with President Taft to save Madero's life . . . the Texas legislature asked Washington to act.

82. In top hat and with the President's ribbon across his chest, General Huerta, accompanied by the gold-braided Blanquet, drove about the sullen capital. The revolution, Ambassador Wilson advised Secretary Knox, was all over. Huerta was in power, things were secure, the Díaz system was nailed back in place. Then, on the night of Washington's Birthday, 1913, Madero and his Vice-President were taken away from the Palace . . . and murdered.

83. Two weeks later a new American President took office. His Secretary of State was William Jennings Bryan. "Usurpations like that of General Huerta," said Mr. Bryan, "menace the peace and development of America as nothing else could. If General Huerta does not retire by force of circumstances, it will become the duty of the United States to use less peaceful means to put him out."

(Bryan and bodyguard on the steps of the State Department, 1913.)

84. By now the great wind was sweeping the country. Carranza, conceded—with some hesitation by the others—to be First Chief, had taken the field . . .

85. Another rebel leader, a former Sonora rancher and mechanic named Álvaro Obregón, was on the move with an "army" . . .
(Obregón is next to the bugler.)

86. Villa was taking one town after another from the Huerta garrisons . . .

87. Within a year these people—Zapatistas, followers of Obregón or Carranza, painters and buglers, Yaqui Indians and mule drivers—had wiped out Huerta's Federal soldiers in three-fourths of Mexico.

88. There was no agreement binding the revolutionaries. There was only a common enemy—Huerta—and a common drive to get a satisfactory place in life. "Death to Huerta, down with the foreigners, Mexico for the Mexicans."

89. There was also revealed an inarticulate set of common hates which could be seen operating when a revolutionary army came to town. Goods were taken from the stores and here the line drawn was between Mexicans and foreigners, but in exact reverse of the distinction made in Díaz days.

(The picture shows Villa's men comparing notes on the plunder taken at Torreón, 1914.)

90. Odd groups gathered around the revolutionary chiefs. Villa had an artist who went along to paint the triumphs of the revolution. The State Department of the United States was represented in the camp by an agent named George Carothers. The Mutual Film Co. came along and offered Villa money to fight a sham battle for movie use. Instead, Villa obliged by hurrying preparations for a real battle and fighting it while the camera crank turned. Villa in his fighting never got beyond the idea of a wild cavalry charge. It was Obregón who learned how to plan a battle, learned how to organize a war, recognized the explosive power behind the revolution and learned how to direct it.

(A council of war in August, 1914. This was one of the few meetings between Obregón and Villa. Third from the left is Obregón. The man in the Stetson and light suit, leaning on his elbow, is Fierro, Villa's "personal killer." The man with the spectacles in the camp chair, leaning against the tent pole, is George Carothers. Villa is just to the right of him.)

91. The main battles were along the railroads. When these armies moved it was like a mass migration . . .

92. . . . whole families went along . . .

93. . . . men, women, and children . . .

94. . . . makeshift shelters of blankets, packing boxes rigged on top of the train
. . . with here and there an umbrella to keep off the sun . . .

95. Children served as runners, sentries or even soldiers . . . Most of the Mexican leaders of today began their careers in these armies of the revolution . . .

96. Lázaro Cárdenas, for example, who left his home town of Jiquilpan when he was fifteen to join Madero's army, and who became President of Mexico twenty-four years later!

97. By April, 1914, Huerta was left with only a small piece of Mexico—the capital and the gulf oil coast. British, Germans, Dutch, and Americans were jockeying for position in the European war that was being prepared and was soon to break. There were incidents, some American marines were seized and . . . Americans under Admiral Fletcher seized and occupied Veracruz. "We are invaded! *¡Viva México! Death to the gringos! ¡Qué viva la revolución!*" By July, 1914, Huerta was an exile . . .

98. . . . living at Forest Hills, Long Island. In 1916 he died in a Texas jail, while scheming to get back to Mexico . . .

99. Carranza was really First Chief now. The revolution was over, said he, and all the boys except those needed for a standing army could begin turning in their guns and go back to work. But the revolutionary chiefs and their boys did not see in the bony, elderly man with the long white beard, the Saint Peter to their heaven. He was First Chief by their will, for their benefit. They had started with nothing . . .

100. . . . their dead were scattered all over Mexico . . .

101. . . . they had broken the yoke themselves and now the good things of Mexican life would be theirs . . . starting at once. Else, what was a revolution?

102. Carranza's answer was—Obey! Obedience was not forthcoming. Obregón arranged a convention at Aguascalientes, half way between the Villa and Carranza camps. The breach between the two men could not be bridged. Obregón sided with Carranza and the war began again. The word was: "You must choose between Villa and Carranza." The war lasted five years . . .

103. . . . Zapata's boys swarmed over the cornfields of Morelos, their women with them . . . seizing the haciendas, breaking open the safes and burning the deeds and the papers . . . Land! Land! Land!

104. Zapata kept on saying, "I'll disband my boys as soon as the land is divided. What are you going to do?"

105. Mexico City was No Man's Land. One day Zapata and his men made a triumphal entry. It was thought that the Attila of the South would butcher the people, but he did not and, after a little while, moved out again.

106. Generals swept in and out and no one could be sure at any time who was supposed to be sitting in the presidential chair . . . and most of the time no one was . . .

107. One day Carranza and his staff were photographed standing in front of it . . .

108. Villa had his picture taken lolling in it, with Zapata beside him . . .

109. It settled down into a decisive duel between Villa and Obregón, who was supporting Carranza. There was a series of fast and sharp engagements and by 1915 Villa was penned in the northern deserts. It was at Santa Rosa, one of the last battles in this duel, that Obregón's right arm was blown off by a grenade.

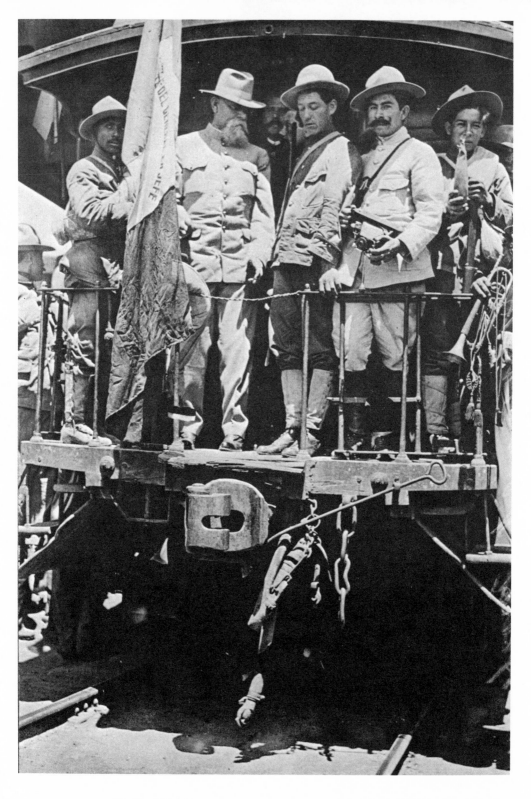

110. Finally Washington recognized Carranza. But now, indeed, the stiffnecked lawyer-rancher-general was in a fix. He had made promises. Zapata kept saying, "What are you going to do about the land?" while his boys kept on seizing haciendas.

III. Villa, still restless, made a carefully planned raid over the river and shot up
Columbus, New Mexico. Pershing was sent after him . . .

112. . . . through the canyons and across the northern desert. The expedition came
to nothing while Carranza wrangled . . . now with Washington . . . now with the
boys . . .

113. In 1917 Carranza tried to put a fence around the revolution by calling a convention at Querétaro to amend the constitution that Benito Juárez and his men had written half a century before and which had been riddled and crippled by Strong Man Díaz. The convention met; it was solemnly addressed by old Moses. Then the followers of Obregón and Zapata and the labor delegates went to work. When they got through they had presented Mexico with the first revolutionary state charter of modern times. Its theory was: All land and other productive resources belong to the commonwealth, but may be held as private property except when public interest requires otherwise.

114. There was plenty of public money, for oil was booming. Most of those close to the top grabbed. Though Carranza was honest, his administration was bogged in corruption. Still from the villages came the cry: "Land! Land!" . . . What had happened to the revolution?

115. Carranza sent his General González to make a deal with Zapata. (González at
the table in panama hat and spectacles; Zapata, in the big white hat, is sitting at
the right.) Zapata was adamant. Since negotiation accomplished nothing, murder
was next in the order of business. On April 10, 1919, Zapata was ambushed and
killed. His body was exhibited and the public bidden, but to this day there are
some who say: He is alive . . . he was seen in the mountains . . . riding alone.

116. The boys began mustering around Obregón, and Carranza prepared for flight. He gathered up the government and the treasury and the few soldiers who remained faithful and put them aboard special trains and started for Veracruz. Simultaneously eight thousand men started from Veracruz to intercept the trains. At a little place called Rinconada one of the trains was wrecked. There was a fight and Carranza and a few followers got away. Three nights later, May 21, 1920, he was killed as he lay sleeping on the floor of a mud hut.

117. They brought him back to Mexico City and buried him . . .

118. . . . and the one-armed General Obregón was duly elected to succeed him. Somehow it seemed as though the revolution had triumphed at last. It was a spring world. The wise-cracking Obregón played with children in the parks . . .

119. Painters shucked into overalls to put the meaning of the revolution, thrice human size, on public walls . . .

(Painting the murals at the School of Agriculture at Chapingo. Diego Rivera is sitting on the scaffolding at the left.)

120. Villa, his last flickers of rebellion dampened with cash and a ranch presented by the government, retired and took it easy.

121. The land, exploding into bloom wherever water touched it, was to be divided up at last. Well, anyhow . . . a start would be made . . .

122. The revolution having been "consolidated," Obregón's government went to work. He organized his cabinet and administration in a way that has been followed ever since. Two or three of the profitable ministries and top posts were reserved to generals, who passed the work along to somebody else. The rest of the cabinet were civilians. One of the most alert and especially concerned with his own future was Plutarco Elías Calles. (Sitting at Obregón's right.) He had been a schoolteacher when he joined Madero's army. He had also been a bartender—and a tough one. Obregón had his hands full. There was not only that cry of Land! to be looked to . . . the railroads were broken down and bankrupt, the customers were mostly pledged to pay interest on the foreign debt. Where was the money coming from to pay for those promised schools, farm machinery . . . roads . . .

123. . . . and village water systems? Water is the most precious of all things in Mexico. It would take millions to carry out the promises. Where was the money coming from for the inevitable "service charges" and cuts to "friends"? There was oil tax money but it wouldn't go far. The few industries—mines, oils, textiles— were foreign owned. Taxes couldn't be raised there without provoking international incidents. No question about it, there would have to be a loan . . . and that meant recognition.

124. Albert B. Fall, United States Secretary of the Interior, was the Mexican expert of the Harding Administration. He put on the screws. If Obregón wanted to be recognized, then he must return to Díaz conditions . . . with extras. That is, unmake the revolution. Obregón said he hadn't the power to make such conditions. It was a fact; he couldn't. His boys were watching every move he made . . . The situation was tense and for a little while it looked as though the Americans were going to move in and take over the place, but in the end, through the efforts of an American banker named John Glenn, who had lived in Mexico for many years and knew what the revolution was all about, the demands from Americans were whittled down. Obregón's government was recognized . . . but he got no loan.

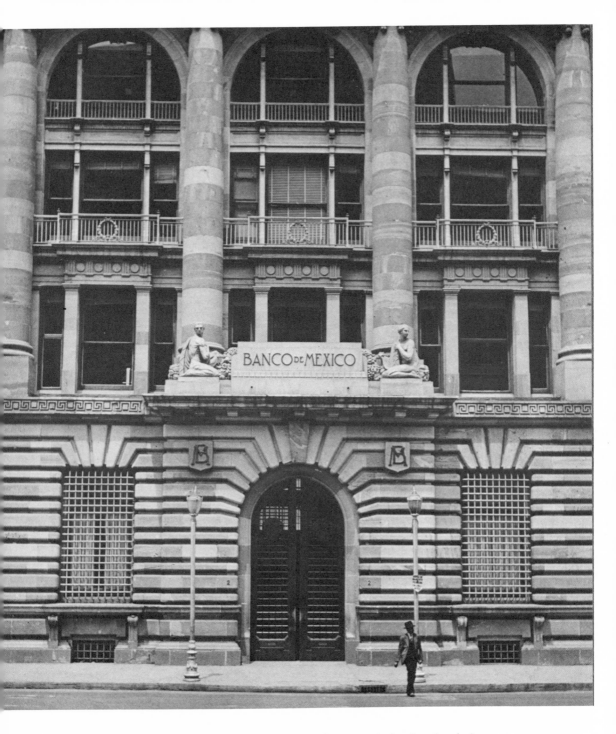

125. Then an idea glimmered through and the idea proved the first break in Mexico's dilemma. Get money where bankers get it . . . in banking. A national bank, government controlled, to finance government enterprises was set up, with private bank money in it . . . or else!

Having made a start with Obregón, the great question in 1924 was: "Who will carry on?" There was no one who could match Obregón as a military leader, as a man of advanced political ideas . . . nor compare with him in personal popularity and political resource.

Violent death cut down three powerful candidates. After the election the defeated candidate rebelled in arms. In the end the prize went to . . .

126. . . . the rocky-jawed ex-bartender, ex-school teacher, Plutarco Elías Calles. Honest government, said he, was to be the watchword. He was inaugurated December 1, 1924.

127. One of the chief reasons for Calles' election was the fact that he had a written contract with the soft-spoken, strong-arm labor boss . . . Luis Morones. The unions had come ahead fast and Morones, aided by his gunmen, had put them together into a tight political machine for the express purpose of electing Calles. In return, Morones was to be made Minister of Labor and Industry.

128. The focus of activity shifted to Morones' new Ministry of Labor. His federation of unions was the *Confederación Regional Obrera Mexicana*—Regional Federation of Mexican Labor—popularly known as the CROM. The double position of government man and union head gave Morones decisive power to roll up CROM membership, to enforce the closed shop in CROM plants, and to cripple unions outside the CROM.

(Parade of the hotel workers union, a CROM organization.)

129. While Morones was busy with his unions, Calles built up his personal machine. His astute economic advisers were busily promoting government-in-business and business-in-government by way of the new banks. More roads were built and work was begun on a series of dams.

(The Calles Dam near Aguascalientes.)

130. There was a business boom and the Mexico City Country Club, sacred to the foreigner in Díaz days, had a new guest list. The old-style roistering generals, accustomed to shoot the necks off cognac bottles in congenial saloons, were metamorphosed into something more social. They played polo and their cars could be seen drawn up under the Country Club awning . . .

131. Calles gave the hand of his daughter Alicia to Jorge Almada, one of the richest young men in Mexico.
   (Calles stands at the bride's right.)

132. He demonstrated his interest in the land question by acquiring a great hacienda and stocking it with the best American farm machinery. He was photographed leaning against a tractor . . . as though to say, "Where your treasure is, there will your heart be also."

What had happened to the revolution? It was plain as daylight that Calles, Morones & Co. would have to step on it to show the people that the election promises meant something. Morones was leading the life of Riley, sporting diamonds and fast cars. Other friends were in the big money. Some kind of action seemed necessary . . . to prove to the waiting boys that the revolution still breathed.

So the Mexican Congress went to work to write the "regulatory" legislation that would put the teeth into the Constitution, a document that was still largely a dead letter. This provoked consternation in Washington. Secretary of State Kellogg said shrilly that "Mexico was on trial before the world." While this dog fight was going on, by a coincidence frequently observed in Mexican politics . . .

133. . . . a Church conflict broke out too. The most powerful cleric in the conflict with Calles was Archbishop Pascual Díaz of Mexico City. This conflict was an old one; it had smouldered for generations. The Church's wealth had been enormous and its hold on the cultural life of the people all-pervasive. Now, said the clerics, the priesthood will not submit to that part of the new Constitution that brings the number of the priesthood and their nationality under government control.

134. The conflict grew more bitter. The Church opposition to popular grade schools run by the government was implacable. In turn there were derisive parades . . . a dead buzzard suspended from a placard that read "Here Comes the Archbishop of Mexico."

135. The breach widened. In July, 1926, the Church suspended religious exercises. Throngs in the churches prayed without the sacrament. Masses became a bootleg article, performed at the risk of a raid. The fight became murderous. Guerrillas called *cristeros* raided the rural schools and left bodies of teachers labeled with banners and placards that said "Christ is King."

(A group of *cristeros* gathered for secret devotions.)

136. No quarter was given in the Church conflict. A plot to murder Obregón was uncovered. Calles sent the suspects to the firing squad.

(The dummies were employed for firing squad practice.)

137. The uproar of the Church fight, the struggle with the oil companies, the old and perpetual arguments with gringo investors had the State Department at Washington by the ears. The cry of intervention was raised once more, but Americans had got tired of these arguments and Congress refused to get excited. Instead President Coolidge sent Dwight Morrow as Ambassador in the fall of 1927 (Morrow, left; Secretary of State Kellogg, right) to try sweet reason on the debt, the oil, the Church, the land, and the labor troubles.

138. But the Mexican people knew that, as far as they were concerned, Calles hadn't delivered and he knew they knew it. As his term ran out it was obvious that no henchman of Calles could be elected President and hold the job very long. The only man with enough prestige and competence to ensure peace with hope was the one-armed veteran Obregón. According to Mexican law, no President may stand for re-election, so an emergency law was passed and an agreement was reached. (Obregón left, Calles right.) The veteran was elected.

139. On the 17th of July, 1928, ten days before the inauguration, all the key men of the *gran familia revolucionaria*, the leading survivors of the heterogeneous groups who had overthrown Porfirio Díaz and made the revolution, gathered in a hall in San Ángel, a suburb of Mexico City, to banquet the hero. (Obregón, with bow tie and spectacles, sits in the center.) A seedy young man drifted in, making caricatures of the guests. Nobody paid attention. Art on the spot is often peddled like songs and lottery tickets in eating and drinking places. The young man hovered near Obregón; he nudged in, slipped his hand into his shoddy black coat, and fired. Obregón pitched over, dying.

(The photo was taken about five minutes before the shot.)

140. The public learned from a trial that filled the front pages for many days, that the killer's name was León Toral (on the right with bow tie) and that he was a member of a terrorist group that had decided that Christ the King required the sacrifice of someone's life for Obregón's. Toral was executed. The Church conflict burst out again.

141. Close-mouthed Emilio Portes Gil, Secretary of the Interior, assumed the Provisional Presidency as the law establishes. The sudden death of Obregón had plunged the opposition into confusion and the Calles machine was left intact. Portes Gil, an extremely adroit administrator, ran the government with Calles' backing. As in the United States, where the great stock market boom roared to its height, so in Mexico the henchmen of Calles rallied for a last burst of prosperity . . .

142. There was a boom in resort real estate. In Cuernavaca, where once Carlotta and Maximilian had wandered in the romantic Borda gardens . . .

143. . . . there sprang up a row of Hollywood mansions inhabited by the big boys.
It was nicknamed Ali Baba Street.

144. In this atmosphere Ambassador Morrow went to work, laboring assiduously to erase the memory of former envoys whose overbearing arrogance had so infuriated the Mexicans. Before a background of Mexican and United States flags—with a photograph of Coolidge to give a sort of benediction—Morrow addressed banquets. He admired the work of Mexican painters and bought their pictures. He applied himself to the oil and Church deadlocks, persuading the parties aggrieved by the Constitution to submit to its laws. In return, it was understood, their application would rest lightly . . .

145. But there was forever the question of land. If the revolution had promised anything, it had promised land. The longing gnawed at the peasants and roused their never-sleeping fear and wrath. Wasn't the memory of Zapata revered because he had said, "Boys, take it, it's yours"? Had not Obregón sworn that the peasants should have the land? Had not every Mexican revolutionary chief chanted the land slogans until they were all but biblical texts? But Calles said the agrarian program had been a failure, that in due course the haciendas would partition themselves, on easy payments. Partition themselves! Peasants who were dissatisfied with this dubious hope were "pacified" . . . by troops . . . sometimes pacified forever . . .

146. The full effects of the world depression belatedly struck Mexico in 1932, choking the exports on which so much of the economic life of the country depended. There were panics, scares . . . runs on the Bank of Mexico.

The Calles group had wrung the last drop of sufferance out of the Mexican people during the administrations that followed the death of Obregón. By 1933 "the great 80%" had their vision and their feelings in focus. The Calles group had a choice: They could set up an oldfashioned terrorist military dictatorship, financed from the United States, or they could sheer to the wind.

147. Hesitating, backing and filling, the Calles group picked a dark horse whom nobody knew much about—General Lázaro Cárdenas. He had fought in the revolutionary ranks and later, as governor of the state of Michoacán, got himself a reputation for building schoolhouses and enforcing the land laws.

(Cárdenas receiving an Indian delegation.)

148. He campaigned for the presidency as if in war . . . fast . . . getting his car over the roughest roads . . . and beyond that on horseback.
   (Cárdenas on the left.)

149. Duly elected, he kept on traveling, as if still campaigning. When President Cárdenas arrived in a village, he came unannounced. He would sit in the town house for ten hours a day . . . listening. People came to present flowers and tell him about the things they desperately needed. Every night the list of needs was made up . . . a pump, a bridge, an orphan of a revolutionary soldier to be sent to school . . . and *land!*

150. Now, and at last, there was really fast action on the land question. The ten per cent of acreage that had been figured the maximum to be distributed was nearly doubled. Land division was the occasion of wild local celebrations . . . In October, 1936, President Cárdenas went in person to divide the land in the Laguna cotton district in Coahuila and Durango. In 1930 there were 130 holdings in this district, mainly owned by Spanish, British, German, and North American companies. The Cárdenas division distributed 220,000 acres to 31,000 families numbering more than 150,000 persons.

151. There were agricultural fairs and model farm demonstrations . . .

152. . . . road building was pushed and hurried ahead . . .

153. The government set up a sugar refinery at Zacatepec in Morelos and, when they named it, invoked one of the great myths . . . Emiliano Zapata.

154. When the peasants discovered that the officials of a local farm bank were grafting, a deputation would wait upon Cárdenas and he would try to help them.

155. Actions of this character had caused the retired Calles much sour reflection. At his home in Cuernavaca he began to rumble out warnings. Cárdenas wasted no time. Calles was pulled out of bed one night—he was supposed to be in the middle of reading *Mein Kampf*—bundled into a plane, and flown across the border into California exile.

156. This was the sort of Chief Executive Mexico had when, in March, 1937, the oil companies refused to make terms with the unions on renewal contracts.

The dispute brought the oil conflict to a final showdown. For more than a generation this struggle between the foreign oil companies and the Mexican government had been a burning question. Porfirio Díaz and the *científicos* had granted unbelievable concessions to Lord Cowdray, to Edward Doheny, to Standard Oil. Later came Harry Sinclair and Royal Dutch. Long before, when the Juárez Constitution was written, all sub-soil wealth had been declared the property of the nation. It might be leased, but never sold outright. There was a tradition behind this that went back to the edicts of the Spanish crown. This tradition Díaz had done away with, and when the Carranza convention at Querétaro in 1917 began rewriting the Constitution, they returned to the ancient doctrine and declared the sub-soil wealth to be national property. The oil companies said: No, and continued, year after year, to say: No.

They now said that they could not meet the unions' demands. Cárdenas offered to set aside the sum in escrow, as a guarantee that the cost would not go above what his experts said. Said the companies: We cannot and will not pay. The dispute finally reached the Mexican Supreme Court, which decided against them. The companies refused to submit. The question now was: Who is boss?

157. Cárdenas knew the oil fields at first hand and when, at last, the final great question was put, he did not hesitate. On March 18, 1938, he declared the oil situation was a national emergency and, in the name of common welfare against private interest, expropriated the wells and refineries.

158. The oil companies roared with anger. Mr. Owen St. Clair O'Malley, the British Ambassador, behaved so arrogantly that two months later, on May 13, 1938, the Mexican government broke relations with Great Britain. "A diplomatic novelty," said the London *Times*. Quivering with rage, Mr. O'Malley announced that he was going home . . .

159. The whole nation seethed with excitement. It was a declaration of independence at last. There were parades in the towns, the crowds milled through the Plaza in Mexico City.

160. In the midst of the tumult there occurred a still greater sensation. The old archbishop of the *cristero* days was dead and, in his stead, Archbishop Luis Martínez, appointed in February, 1937, presided over the Mexican hierarchy. Sensing the unanimity of feeling and seeking some way to make terms in the Church conflict, Martínez urged all Mexicans to stand by their government in the oil crisis.

161. This time there was no chance of intervention from Washington. By a strange accident, the United States Ambassador—a newspaper editor from Raleigh, North Carolina—was the same man who as Secretary of the Navy in 1914 had ordered Admiral Fletcher to seize Veracruz. But things were different now. Mr. Daniels had come down to try out the Good Neighbor Policy and did not propose to advise landing the Marines.

(Daniels in the middle, talking to Cárdenas at a New Year's Day reception. Mr. Daniels didn't drink the champagne in his glass. Mr. Stephen Aguirre, on the right, the Third Secretary at the American Embassy, did it for him.)

162. Great indeed were the changes since the days of Don Porfirio. Young men now could earn the incredible sum of $1.20 a day in the Moctezuma Brewery at Orizaba . . .

163. Where once there were only wooden plows, now some of the peasants had plows with steel points . . .

164. . . . where an ambitious young man in the Díaz days had longed, without hope, for a career, now he might be a lawyer arguing cases for employers . . .

165. . . . or a lawyer arguing cases for unions . . .

166. More folks had better clothes than they had had in other days and, when the itinerant photographer took their pictures, they could have an airplane background if they wanted it . . .

167. The bus line from Cuautla—where the body of the murdered Zapata had been displayed for show—passed through the village of Amecameca, where there was a public school now, made out of a church and named after the ex-president, ex-barkeeper, Calles . . .

168. Cárdenas was an observer of a situation even more unbelievable than in the Díaz days . . . a textile plant, built in the last months of the Díaz era, was now the scene of a struggle between two unions for control. One was the remnant of the CROM. The other was led by . . .

169. . . . Lombardo Toledano, once a lieutenant of Luis Morones, and now a great union boss himself. After the murder of Obregón, the props had been pulled from under the CROM by Portes Gil. The power of the CROM had waned and out of the strength of the unions that had bucked Morones, Toledano had built a federation greater than the CROM had ever been . . .

170. The top machinery of the unions was Communist controlled . . .

171. . . . and John L. Lewis, then president of the C. I. O., came down to Mexico City to address them.

(Toledano is sitting at the table, second from the right.)

172. The face of Mexico City had been changed since the days of the *científicos* and their cake-frosting French mansard architecture.

173. On the doors of German consulates a symbol had appeared, as sinister as the uniform of the *rurales* had ever been in the old days . . .

174. In 1940 General Ávila Camacho was picked as the candidate of the official government party. A strange sort of twilight was descending on Mexico. Where the Nazis were not busy—organizing the German commercial element and ladling out the cash—their friends, the sympathizers of the Spanish dictator Franco, were pushing the cause of an organization called the Spanish Falange. The declared purpose of this organization was to tie Mexico and South America to the Fascist kite. Toledano and the Communists, who had ridden high, wide, and handsome, were on the defensive and losing ground. As for the great body of Mexicans, about all they could do was to hope for the best, hope that the advantages so hardly won in a generation of revolutionary turmoil would not be swept away by the European hurricane.

If Cárdenas was troubled about the future, at any rate he finally signified that he would support General Ávila Camacho. (Left to right: General Eduardo Hay, one of the Madero revolutionists; General Ávila Camacho; President Cárdenas; and General Magaña. Magaña is a veteran of Zapata's guerrilla army.) Would General Ávila Camacho uphold, cherish, and sustain the principles of the revolution? Well . . . no doubt. At any rate, he could reassure the State Department at Washington that the Good Neighbor Policy was being watched over, and, well, nobody was going to rock the boat.

175. His opponent was General Juan Almazán. Did he undertake to uphold, cherish, and sustain the principles of the revolution? On the one hand . . . yes. At any rate, he wouldn't rock the boat either. He would reassure capital, but he would not give way to the oil companies. He was supported by political Catholics, but still he had his picture taken passing out the dividends at the co-operative store at Monterrey.

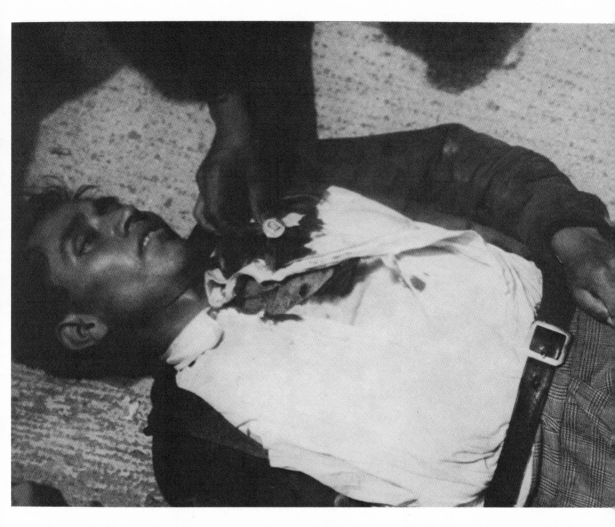

176. The campaign was bloody and confused. On the one hand, the official party was the party of Cárdenas, whose popularity was undimmed. That was help for General Ávila Camacho. On the other hand, thousands of Mexicans, union members and peasants included, were sick to death of the government rackets, the union rackets, the grafting, and the sight of an overloaded political gravy train.

Election day was the signal for violence everywhere. Some voters, their candidates' buttons displayed, never lived to reach the polls. At the end of the day Cárdenas made the rounds of the polls and saw the worst and said: "Mexico is not yet a democracy." The official candidate was declared elected . . . but nobody ever knew whether he was or not.

177. Meantime the European upheaval had sent back to Mexico a strange crew of personages who hadn't been seen in more than a generation. The Widow Díaz, like some wraith recalled from the past, was back again, receiving guests with much pomp. The heirs . . . and assigns . . . of the ancient *científicos* were coming back . . . investing in real estate and looking very busy. There was a boom and the price of living began to rise. Americans were getting interested again. William Randolph Hearst, one of the most vociferous clamorers for intervention in other days, descended once more on Mexico City and was received by the President.

178. There was a revival of splendid entertaining at the National Palace in a style that had not been seen in years . . .

179. In the wake of the Spanish Falange propaganda, there arose a peasant league, formed around the old *cristeros*, peasants from the big haciendas. These peasants called themselves *sinarquistas* . . . organized with a blend of Nazi and Franco slogans. Everywhere feeling grew more tense, more nervous . . . all the old influences, the attitudes and arguments, of the Díaz era, seemed to be coming back in a wave . . . plus.

180. On June 1, 1942, the Mexican government declared war against the Axis. Most Mexicans were thunderstruck. In the towns they gathered in front of movie houses and stores to listen to the loud speakers announcing that President Ávila Camacho had taken them into the war. What were they doing, fighting on the same side as the United States . . . pointing their guns *with* the Yanquis and not *at* them? Was any good going to come of this?

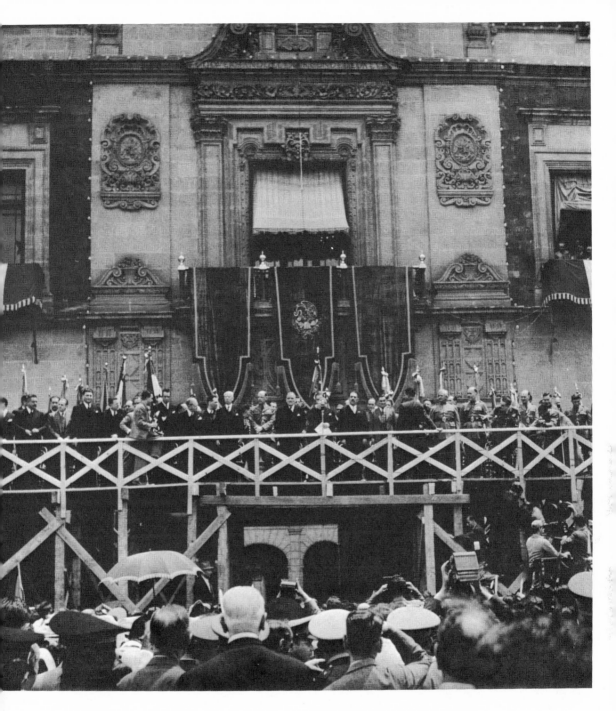

181. Then came an astounding occurrence. On Independence Day, September 16, 1942, at the ceremonies there appeared on the reviewing stand before the National Palace . . . on the very spot where the aged Don Porfirio had reviewed his last parade so long ago . . . *all the living ex-presidents of Mexico* to ask for loyal support of the war! Strange spectacle. Calles, home from exile, older but still looking like a tough-jawed bartender; Cárdenas, the incendiary who ousted the oil men; Portes Gil with the tight mouth, looking neither to left nor right; Rodríguez and Ortiz Rubio, the short term president who had "the personality of a ship's purser." And in the center, General Ávila Camacho with the opulent chin, reassuring all and sundry that no one would rock the boat.

182. That night the Cathedral was magnificently illuminated . . . there was a Te Deum. The nation was at war . . . for Democracy, the posters said . . .

183. Well, maybe so. Maybe it was all right to go to war along with the gringos, but veterans who had fought with Obregón had long and troubled thoughts. They had fought to make a revolution . . . the schools that so many villages were still waiting for . . . the water and the land? Some had got theirs but others were still waiting. And the boys . . .

184. . . . who had grown up with the idea that the revolution would somehow make their future. Would they lose it all . . . or was the prospect still fair and bright . . . would Mexico some day belong to the Mexicans?

The Photographic History of the Mexican Revolution

UP TO THE OUTBREAK of the Mexican Revolution in 1910, news photography was a simple and untroubled business. The regular assignments of news photographers could be accommodated in six neat compartments: sports, stage people, politicians, society, American businessmen, and European crowned heads and nobilities. The demand for the last named was endless; the American public had an apparently inexhaustible appetite for pictures of Manuel of Portugal, the Duchess of Manchester (neé Zimmerman of Cincinnati), and the daughters of Nicholas of Montenegro. Occasionally a news story would get a thorough going over with a camera—the anthracite strike of 1902, a wreck on the New York Elevated, the San Francisco earthquake, Mrs. Pankhurst in Holloway Gaol—but not often.

The business of the news photographer was to show, anonymously and as expertly as possible, a world in place. The few news photographers who traveled far and wide—men like Jack Hamment, Jimmy Hare, and Herbert Ponting—were almost celebrities themselves, ranked with correspondents like Richard Harding Davis. Even they were a comparatively recent phenomenon. The common use of halftone reproduction of photographs was unknown until the 90's—the first halftone used by the New York *Tribune* was a picture of Tom Platt published January 21, 1897—and the notion of news photography was so startling that Hare had difficulty in persuading *Collier's* to send him to Cuba in 1898. Hearst was more alert and Hare's great rival through the Spanish War was Jack Hamment of the New York *Evening Journal*. But Hare's success was so remarkable that he was promptly translated into an attraction, a man who traveled the lyceum circuits when he wasn't photographing the Russo-Japanese War and other international disturbances. All through the boom years of the muckrake periodicals after 1900, most of the photographs were "scenes" or posed photographs of notables.

All this changed abruptly upon the outbreak of the Mexican Revolution. There had been two years of warning that "something was going to happen" in Mexico—Mexican historians frequently date the revolution from March, 1908, when *Pearson's Magazine* published the famous Creelman interview with Díaz. If the picture agencies didn't grasp all the story when Minister of the Treasury Limantour arrived in New York from Paris in January, 1911, they knew there was a story there and had a photographer at the Plaza Hotel to get it and they had men across town at the Astor Hotel to photograph the Maderos. Trouble was expected at the border and a number of United States regiments had been mustered at San Antonio. Jack Ironson, sports photographer for International, was with the Giants on their spring trip when he was advised by wire to proceed to Mexico and get pictures of the trouble. While he was mulling over this strange assignment, he got another wire: "Quit dodging baseballs and start dodging bullets."

Even though they didn't know it, the news photographers were getting set to grapple with a social upheaval. If the span of years of the Mexican Revolution is accepted as it is given in this volume, then it is fair to say that no revolution has ever been so thoroughly photographed. The bulk of the picture making was done either by news photographers in line of duty or by individuals who were either participants or spectators and had a particular interest in what was going on. According to W. A. Willis, the New York *Herald* correspondent, "The place was lousy with free lance photographers." The names of most of these people are lost, their pictures scattered. The newsmen were not "artists" but simply photographers earning a living; few of the others had any idea that their pictures would be reproduced. To some of the newsmen—this was before the day when correspondents had economic interpretation on tap at all hours—the revolution was a powerful jolt. One of them says, "Do you know why the Mexicans started that revolution? It was because most of them were slaves."

Jimmy Hare was at San Antonio, taking pictures of the plane that Robert Collier had given the army, when rumors of trouble on the border reached him. He got to El Paso on May 9, 1911. With a reporter from the Omaha *Bee* and "a local photographer named Kiefer" he made his way across the bridge to Juárez that night, avoiding the newspapermen congregated on the American side. So little was stirring that he concluded that the Madero revolution had been overadvertised and wired *Collier's* to that effect. But the next day, when he returned to Juárez, he found that fighting had broken out in earnest. After a number of adventures he was told that there was a big argument going on just outside of town in the "Peace Grove" and that Madero didn't want to fight any longer. He proposed to send a flag of truce to General Navarro, commander of the Díaz garrison, and ask permission to carry away the dead. Presently, Hare, who had taken refuge from snipers in a barroom, was roused by a man going by outside, plastered with Red Crosses and carrying a white flag. This was Madero's envoy. Hare discovered him to be Gerald Brandon, a photographer from Panama (No. 120 is one of Brandon's pictures), and got Brandon's consent to go along. As he and Brandon were returning from their errand, they were startled by firing and wild yelling from another part of town. General Navarro believed himself to be in control of the situation and it was this unexpected attack—the first revolutionary appearance of Francisco Villa—that resulted in the capture of the town and formally set the revolution going. Hare, the celebrity, got his pictures but new-style competition was close behind him.

Robert Dorman, now (1943) the General Manager of Acme News Pictures in New York City, was an example. As Dorman tells the story, in December, 1910, he was a clerk in the Cleveland office of the American Steel and Wire Company and fed up with his job. On New Year's Day, 1911, he went down to the depot, shoved a $100 bill through the wicket, and asked for as much transportation as that would buy. After some figuring the agent calculated that first class accommodations to El Paso would come to about $99. When Dorman arrived in El Paso he discovered that there was a revolution about to break across the Rio Grande. "I crossed the border," he says, "two weeks ahead of Madero."

Dorman went as an adventurer and joined one of the guerrilla bands. (No. 59 is a photograph by Dorman of one of the guerrilla camps.) He had had some experience as an amateur photographer and from the start took pictures for his own interest. (No. 68, the picture of the snipers at Juárez, was taken by Dorman, who didn't know that Hare or Brandon or other news photographers were there.) Presently he discovered that he could do better by himself as a photographer than as a guerrilla. Forming a partnership with E. C. Aultman, a photographer of El Paso, Dorman set out seriously to photograph the progress of the revolution in northern Mexico. (No. 47 of Madero is Dorman's work.) Later on he acquired and fitted up a freight car and this car, hitched to Villa's trains, moved about following the fighting. He was a companion of John Reed's in Villa's famous advance on Torreón and was present at the fight at Gómez Palacio.

Like most of the other revolutionary chieftains, Villa was partial to photographers and cameramen from the Mutual Film Company, and other early moving picture outfits were received with great hospitality. Reed and many of the correspondents took pictures themselves. At one time, during the months when the revolutionary water was being muddied by the fight between the Maderistas and the followers of Pascual Orozco (Orozco is one of the group in No. 75), Reed was entertained by General Urbina. Some reciprocal gesture seemed called for, so, says Reed, "For the next hour I took photographs of General Urbina: General Urbina on foot, with and without sword; General Urbina on three different horses; General Urbina with and without his family; General Urbina's three children, on horseback and off; General Urbina's mother, and his mistress; the entire family, armed with swords and revolvers, including the phonograph, produced for the purpose, one of the children holding a placard upon which was inked: 'General Tomás Urbina R.' "

Still another sort of photographer was Edward Larocque Tinker, best known for his books about Louisiana. Tinker had not only traveled about Mexico in the Díaz days, but on a number of occasions spent his vacations following cattle drives south of the border. When the revolution broke he went along for a time as a spectator. Presently he attached himself to Obregón's army as a sort of fellow traveler and assistant to the hospital corps. This was something of a task, for Obregón's armies, though never beaten in battle, were usually smaller than those of the enemy and the care of the wounded was a heavy job. It was after a fight at Cabullona in

Sonora that Obregón woke Tinker early in the morning in order that the General and his bugler (No. 85) might be photographed on the spot where the fight had been hottest the day before.

The occupation of Veracruz was photographed by a number of American photographers, including Hare and Harris. Hare believes that his photos, taken above Veracruz harbor in one of the early army planes, are among the first if not the first news pictures taken from the air. Villa's raid on Columbus, New Mexico, brought another contingent of news photo men. William Hearfield, now of the New York *Journal American*, arrived at the office for work one morning, was handed a supply of film and told to go. Among those who went down at the time were Eddie Jackson, now of the New York *Daily News*, Homer Scott, William Durbrough, Carl Helm, Victor Kubes of International, William Fox, now a captain in the Air Force, and others. Some of the photographs of Carranza in this volume are believed to have been the work of Ashton Duff, a legendary news photographer who was killed in a taxi smashup in New York twenty years ago.

Gradually, as the revolution went on, the picture making was more systematically organized and now almost all photo agencies have picture connections in Mexico. During the days of the "Mexican Renaissance," photographers by the score wandered all over Mexico. Edward Weston, for example, had a studio there and it was his assistant, Tina Modotti, who worked the print of Zapata (No. 71) out of a battered negative, taken originally by some unknown.

Of the Mexican photographers, one of the best known was Casasola. Casasola, the father, was the photographer of *El Imparcial* and was active during the revolutionary period. Of his four sons, all photographers, two now work for *Novedades*, one for *La Prensa*, and the fourth for the Mexican government. Some years ago the father began the collection and publication of photographs of the revolution and since his death the work has been carried on by his sons. Their collection includes not only the work of the Casasola family, but also that of various other Mexican photographers. Fifteen of the pictures in this volume are Casasola pictures and thirteen of them are from a series secured in Mexico City from the Casasola collection by Leah Brenner.

Much assistance was given by Walker Evans in the planning of the book. A number of the prints are his work.

Wherever possible, in the following pages, the photographer is identified as well as the agency handling the pictures. Too many of the names are gone forever.

GEORGE R. LEIGHTON

SOME IMPORTANT DATES IN MEXICAN HISTORY

1520—Conquest of Mexico by Cortés

1810, September 16—Declaration of Mexican Independence by Father Miguel Hidalgo

1821—Recognition of Mexican Independence by Juan O'Donojú, last Spanish viceroy

1836—Texas declares its independence of Mexico

1846–48—Mexican War with the United States

1859—Benito Juárez named President

1861–67—French intervention

1864—Arrival of Emperor Maximilian

1867, June 19—Execution of Maximilian

1867—Juárez elected President

1871—Revolt of General Porfirio Díaz against Juárez

1872—Death of Juárez

1877—Porfirio Díaz named President

1880—General Manuel González elected President

1884–1910—Díaz re-elected continuously

1906, June—The Greene-Cananea Copper Company strike

1907, January 7—Suppression of the Río Blanco strike

1908, March—Publication of the Creelman interview with Díaz in *Pearson's Magazine*

1908—Publication of Francisco I. Madero's *The Presidential Succession*

1909—Publication of Molina Enríquez' *The Great National Problems*

1909, June 20—Risings in Chihuahua and Coahuila set off by Ricardo and Enrique Flores Magón

1910, September—Centennial of Mexican Independence

1911, January 30—Revolt in Lower California headed by Ricardo Flores Magón

1911, March 6—Mobilization of United States Army on Mexican border

1911, May 10—Capture of the city of Juárez by the Maderistas

1911, May 25—Resignation and flight of Díaz

1911, June 7—Madero enters Mexico City

1911, November 28—Emiliano Zapata issues the *Plan de Ayala*

1913, February 9–19—"The Tragic Ten Days" in Mexico City and accession of Victoriano Huerta to the presidency

1913, February 22—Murder of President Madero and Vice-President Pino Suárez

1914, April 2—Capture of Torreón by Francisco Villa

1914, April 21—Seizure of Veracruz by the United States Navy

1914, July 15—Resignation and flight of President Huerta

1914, November 1—The Aguascalientes convention

1915, April 16—Defeat of Villa by Obregón at the battle of Celaya

1916, March 9—Villa's raid on Columbus, New Mexico

1917, February 5—Withdrawal from Mexico of the Pershing Expedition

1917, May 1—Carranza inaugurated as Constitutional President

1917—New Constitution framed at Querétaro

1919, April 10—Murder of Emiliano Zapata

1920, May 21—Murder of President Carranza at Tlaxcalantongo

1920, December 1—Álvaro Obregón inaugurated as President

1923—Expulsion of Monsignor Filippi, papal delegate

1923, July 18—Murder of Francisco Villa

1923, August 31—Obregón's government recognized by the United States

1924, December 1—Plutarco Elías Calles inaugurated as President

1926, January—The Church denounces the religious and educational provisions of the new Constitution

1926, July 31—Religious exercises suspended by the Church

1927, October—Arrival of Dwight Morrow as United States Ambassador

1928—Re-election of Álvaro Obregón

1928, July 17—Assassination of Obregón by José León Toral

1928, December 1—Emilio Portes Gil inaugurated as Provisional President

1930, February 5—Pascual Ortiz Rubio inaugurated as President

1932, September 1—Ortiz Rubio resigns and General Abelardo Rodríguez assumes the Presidency

1933, March 17—Josephus Daniels appointed United States Ambassador to Mexico

1934, November 30—General Lázaro Cárdenas inaugurated as President

1937, February 25—Luis Martínez appointed Archbishop by Pope Pius XI

1938, March 18—President Cárdenas expropriates the foreign-controlled oil fields

1940—Manuel Ávila Camacho elected President

1942, June 1—Mexico declares war on the Axis

SOURCES

In *The Wind That Swept Mexico*, the story of the Mexican Revolution has been put together in English for the first time. There are no complete accounts of it in Spanish, either, so the sources are:

1. Eyewitnesses. The author saw the upheaval as a child, and later knew many of its important participants and learned something about the way it looked to each of them. Its analysts and scholarly participants—such as, for instance, Jesús Silva Herzog, Federico Bach, Ramón Beteta, Eduardo Suárez, José Miguel Bejarano—have taught the author, amiably and patiently, much about the underlying facts and processes.

2. Biographies and memoirs, many written in the midst of struggle and as part of it.

3. General works such as the annual statistics and information compiled by the Mexican government, some for publication, some only for the guidance of its ministries; the United States Department of Commerce's bulletins and yearbooks; United States consular reports, and specific works such as Dr. Eyler Simpson's study of the Mexican land problem (*The Ejido, Mexico's Way Out*); Dr. Ernest Gruening's history of Mexico, on which the author worked as a research assistant; Andrés Molina Enríquez' *Los grandes problemas nacionales* and *La revolución agraria de México*. Much valuable information was also found in James Morton Callahan's *American Foreign Policy in Mexican Relations*, Walter Flavius McCaleb's *The Public Finances of Mexico*, Edgar Turlington's *Mexico and Her Foreign Creditors*, Edward R. Bell's *The Political Shame of Mexico*, and Marjorie Clark's *Organized Labor in Mexico*.

However, if the list of printed sources read and consulted were to be given completely, it would run on page after page tediously; and, since this is no academic history nor Ph.D. thesis, it would add nothing to the story but more space. When the complete history of the Mexican Revolution is written, with unlimited opportunities to check each eyewitness against the other, each printed source against its sources, the details in *The Wind That Swept Mexico* can be amplified and some, maybe, will stand correction. The author does not claim to be infallible. She does know that enough checking and digging has been done, through a good many years, to make her sure that she has arrived at a more complete, accurate, and fair account than has so far been published.

ANITA BRENNER

1. Brown Bros. (Pablo Viau)
2. F. L. Clarke
3. Brown Bros. (F. L. Clarke)
4. Brown Bros. (C. B. Waite)
5. Casasola
6. International
7. International
8. Brown Bros.
9. European Picture Service (Paul Thompson)
10. International
11. Underwood & Underwood
12. Underwood & Underwood
13. Underwood & Underwood
14. Underwood & Underwood
15. Keystone View
16. Fritz Henle
17. Fritz Henle
18. International
19. Underwood & Underwood
20. Brown Bros.
21. International
22. Brown Bros.
23. International
24. Brown Bros.
25. Casasola
26. Brown Bros.
27. Ewing Galloway
28. Brown Bros.
29. Brown Bros.
30. Brown Bros.
31. Brown Bros.
32. Brown Bros.
33. Casasola
34. Casasola
35. Keystone
36. European Picture Service (Paul Thompson)
37. Mexican Travel Bureau
38. Ewing Galloway
39. Steinheimer-Pix
40. Keystone View
41. Unknown
42. Brown Bros.
43. Brown Bros.
44. Casasola
45. Brown Bros.
46. European Picture Service (Paul Thompson)
47. Keystone View (Robert Dorman)
48. Brown Bros.
49. European Picture Service (Paul Thompson)
50. International
51. International
52. International
53. Underwood & Underwood
54. Brown Bros. (Lee)
55. Brown Bros. (Mexican Herald Photo)
56. Brown Bros.
57. Brown Bros.
58. European Picture Service (Paul Thompson)
59. Acme News Pictures (Robert Dorman)
60. International
61. Brown Bros.
62. Underwood & Underwood
63. European Picture Service (Paul Thompson)
64. European Picture Service (Paul Thompson)
65. European Picture Service (Paul Thompson)
66. Underwood & Underwood
67. Brown Bros.
68. Acme News Pictures (Robert Dorman)
69. Underwood & Underwood
70. Keystone View
71. Modotti (from an old negative)
72. Casasola
73. Casasola
74. European Picture Service (Paul Thompson)
75. Brown Bros.
76. Pix (Casasola)
77. Brown Bros.

78. Casasola
79. Underwood & Underwood
80. Casasola
81. Underwood & Underwood
82. Casasola
83. Keystone View
84. International
85. European Picture Service (Edward L. Tinker)
86. Brown Bros.
87. European Picture Service (Paul Thompson)
88. Underwood & Underwood
89. Brown Bros.
90. Brown Bros.
91. Underwood & Underwood
92. Casasola
93. Unknown
94. Unknown
95. Keystone View
96. Unknown
97. Brown Bros.
98. Underwood & Underwood
99. International
100. Brown Bros.
101. Acme News Pictures
102. Underwood & Underwood
103. International (Vargas)
104. International (Vargas)
105. International
106. International
107. International
108. International (rephotographed 1914 by International from an original by Casasola)
109. European Picture Service (Paul Thompson)
110. International
111. Brown Bros.
112. Brown Bros.
113. European Picture Service (Paul Thompson)
114. Ewing Galloway
115. International
116. International
117. International
118. International
119. Unknown
120. Keystone View (Gerald Brandon)
121. Steinheimer-Pix
122. Casasola
123. Mexican Travel Bureau
124. European Picture Service (Paul Thompson)
125. Steinheimer-Pix
126. Keystone View
127. Keystone View
128. Casasola
129. Unknown
130. Steinheimer-Pix
131. European Picture Service (Paul Thompson)
132. Unknown
133. International
134. Keystone View
135. Casasola
136. Ewing Galloway
137. European Picture Service (Paul Thompson)
138. Keystone View
139. Underwood & Underwood
140. European Picture Service (Paul Thompson)
141. Keystone View
142. Fritz Henle
143. Ewing Galloway
144. International
145. Steinheimer-Pix
146. Anita Brenner
147. Steinheimer-Pix
148. Steinheimer-Pix
149. Unknown
150. Julio Sosa
151. Press Association
152. Acme News Pictures
153. Steinheimer-Pix
154. Black Star
155. Acme News Pictures
156. Keystone View
157. Black Star
158. Pix
159. International
160. Acme News Pictures
161. Pix
162. Pix
163. Fritz Henle
164. Steinheimer-Pix
165. Steinheimer-Pix
166. Fritz Henle
167. Ewing Galloway
168. Pix
169. Pix
170. Pix
171. Black Star

172. Ewing Galloway
173. European News Pictures
174. Pix
175. Pix
176. Black Star
177. Press Association
178. Black Star (Calleja)

179. Black Star (Doris Heyden)
180. Pix
181. Pix
182. Pix
183. Monkmeyer (Silberstein)
184. Black Star (Calleja)

INDEX

Light face figures are for references in the text.

Bold face italic figures are for photograph numbers.